STEP-BY-STEP
Christmas Treats

Christmas Treats

Janice Murfitt

Photography by Edward Allwright

SMITHMARK

This edition published in 1994 by
SMITHMARK Publishers Inc.
16 East 32nd Street
New York
NY 10016

SMITHMARK books are available for bulk purchase for sales
promotion and for premium use. For details write or call
the Manager of Special Sales, SMITHMARK Publishers Inc.
16 East 32nd Street, New York, NY, 10016; (212) 532–6600.

ISBN 0 8317 7843 1

Produced by Anness Publishing Limited
1 Boundary Row
London SE1 8HP

Editorial Director: Joanna Lorenz
Series Editor: Lindsay Porter
Designer: Peter Laws
Jacket Designer: Peter Butler
Photographer: Edward Allwright
Stylist: Maria Kelly

Printed and bound by Graphicom S.r.l., Vincenza

CONTENTS

INTRODUCTION

Christmas is such a wonderful time, a time full of excitement and surprises. Every city, town and village enters into the spirit, decorating the streets with brightly colored lights and festive trees, and filling the air with the sound of Christmas carols. Shops are overflowing with Christmas fare, tempting treats and gifts, and there is certainly a magical feeling everywhere.

There is always so much to plan at Christmastime — and organizing and choosing Christmas presents must be near the top of the list. This book is packed full of tempting festive treats that you can make yourself, from cookies, candies, individual puddings and cakes, to savory butters, pâtés and spiced vinegars. We'll show you how to present your treasures in pretty wrapping paper and boxes, to make delightful, delicious presents with a personal touch.

Share the true spirit of Christmas by making your own gifts for friends and family, and make *Step-by-Step Christmas Treats* part of the celebrations.

Equipment

Some of the recipes that follow call for specialized items of equipment to obtain the best results. These are readily available from standard kitchenware suppliers. Look after your equipment well and it should never need replacing. Always ensure that metal cutters, pans and utensils are kept in a warm dry place to prevent any discoloration and store piping nozzles in rigid containers to prevent them from being damaged.

Chopping boards
These are for chopping or rolling out pastry or icing, and can be made of wood or acrylic. Acrylic is non-stick and especially good for working with marzipan, icing and sugar.

Cookie sheets
Good quality steel sheets in different sizes and without sides are best as these will not buckle during cooking.

Cooling racks
Wide and narrow mesh racks in a variety of sizes are needed for drying and cooling cakes, icing, chocolate and glacé fruits.

Cutters
A set of round, oval, square, plain or fluted cutters is necessary for cutting out cookies, pastry or icing shapes.

Flour and sugar dredgers
These are used for lightly dusting surfaces with flour before rolling out doughs and for dredging sugar on top of cakes and pastries.

Flower and leaf cutters
Tiny metal cutters are available in almost any shape or size to match any flower bloom or leaf shape.

Flower mat
This mat is invaluable for giving sugar flowers and leaves a natural shape while working the paste; foam sponge may be used as a substitute.

Food mixers and processors
Large food mixers are good for mixing large cake quantities quickly and thoroughly. They are ideal for chopping and crushing or for making pastry or bread doughs and will cut down on preparation time.

jelly bag

flower mat

modeling tools

measuring cup

measuring cups

paintbrushes

pans

saucepan

preserving jar

spatula

pans

measuring spoons

cooling rack

jam funnel

cookie sheet

flour dredg

rolling pin

grater

potato peeler

knives

flower and leaf cutters

zing brush

sieve

spatulas

cutters

mixing bowls

chopping board

Glazing brushes
Keep a variety of sizes for glazing cakes, brushing pastry and greasing pans. They are available in small, medium and large sizes.

Graters
A 4- or 6-sided grater with a variety of grating sizes is necessary for many ingredients.

Jam funnels
These are made of stainless steel and are invaluable for filling jars with jam, jelly or chutney without spillage or drips. Use narrow funnels for filling bottles.

Jelly bag
A good quality jelly bag with a very fine weave will ensure that the jelly is crystal clear. A stand is useful but you can improvise with an upturned stool or hook.

Knives
Good quality knives are an investment. Choose a long-bladed knife for slicing, a medium one for chopping and a small knife for paring.

Measuring cups
These are useful for measuring dry ingredients. They can be large or small, heatproof or plastic, for accurate measuring of liquids.

Measuring spoons
These are ideal for the consistent measuring of spoon sizes as general spoons vary widely.

Mixing bowls
Keep several different sizes including heatproof bowls, for whisked mixtures and sugar syrup. The insides should have a smooth rounded finish to ensure thorough mixing.

Modeling tools
These are a good investment if you enjoy cake decoration or modeling. The bone tool is needed for making flowers and the scalpel for cutting out shapes. The scribing tool is invaluable for piercing, marking out and outlining.

Muslin
Very fine cotton muslin is invaluable for straining mixtures in place of a jelly bag, for enclosing pickling spices for flavoring or infusing, and for covering icing to keep it from drying out.

Nozzles
Straight-sided, good quality metal piping nozzles will give a good clean result. They are expensive but should not need replacing if treated with care.

Paintbrushes
A wide selection is available from good cake icing and decorating suppliers. Use paintbrushes for painting on food colorings, sticking sugar pieces together with Gum Glaze and for dusting with food coloring dusts.

Palette
This is useful for keeping small quantities of food coloring dusts separate.

Pans
Round, square or jelly roll cake pans and molds should be of the best quality. Good quality metal pans will not bend or warp during cooking and should never need replacing if they are well looked after.

Pencil, eraser and scissors
These are always necessary for drawing around pan sizes on paper, measuring pan sizes and for cutting out paper templates.

Potato peeler
Use to pare rinds from fruit, or chocolate curls off blocks of chocolate.

Rolling pins
Smooth, straight-ended rolling pins made of wood or acrylic are useful for pastry, dough and icing. Acrylic non-stick rolling pins come in several sizes.

Sieves
Small and fine mesh sieves made of wire or nylon are useful for sieving and straining ingredients and mixtures.

Spatulas
These are essential for all types of cooking especially small, crank-handled spatulas for fine icing and sugar work. They are available with small, medium and large blades.

Apricot Glaze

It is always a good idea to make a large quantity of apricot glaze, especially if you need it for a celebration cake.

Makes 2 cups

INGREDIENTS
2 cups apricot jam
2 tbsp water

1 Place the jam and water into a saucepan, and heat gently, stirring occasionally until melted.

2 Boil the jam rapidly for 1 minute, then strain through a sieve. Rub through as much fruit as possible, using a spoon, and discard any skins left in the sieve.

3 Pour the glaze into a clean, hot jar, seal with a clean lid and cool. Store in the fridge where it will keep well for up to 2 months.

Royal Icing

Royal icing will dry very hard. It is ideal for covering cakes and piping decorations.

Makes 2 cups

INGREDIENTS
2 egg whites
¼ tsp lemon juice
2 cups confectioners' sugar, sieved
1 tsp glycerin

1 Place the egg whites and lemon juice into a clean bowl. Stir, using a clean wooden spoon to break up the whites.

2 Add a little of the sugar and mix well until the mixture is the consistency of unwhipped cream. Continue to add small quantities of sugar until the desired consistency has been reached, mixing well between each addition.

3 Stir in the glycerin until the icing is well blended.

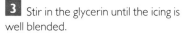

Lining a Deep Cake Pan of any Shape

For rich or light fruit cakes, use good quality fixed-base deep cake pans. Ensure that you have the correct size of pan for the quantity of cake mixture.

1 Place the pan on a piece of double thickness waxed paper or parchment paper and draw around the base following the pan shape. Cut out the marked shape with a pair of scissors.

2 Measure and cut a strip of double thickness waxed paper or parchment paper long enough to wrap around the outside of the pan with a small overlap and deep enough to stand 1 in above the top of the pan.

3 Brush the base and sides of the pan with melted fat or oil. Place the cut-out paper shape in the base of the pan and press flat. Fit the double strip of waxed paper or parchment paper inside the pan, pressing well against the sides and making sharp creases where the paper fits into the corners of the pan. Ensure that the paper strip is level and fits neatly without any creases. Brush the base and sides well with melted fat or oil.

4 Measure and fit a double thickness strip of brown paper around the outside of the pan. Tie securely with string.

5 Line a cookie sheet with several layers of brown paper and stand your prepared cake pan in the center.

Templates

For gingerbread houses, you may find it easier to use a template for the walls and roof of the house.

1 Draw the dimensions required onto stiff card, and cut out. Position on top of the rolled out dough, and cut around the card shape with a pair of scissors or sharp knife.

Preparing Containers for Preserves

It is most important that the containers used to hold preserves have no cracks or chips which could harbour micro-organisms and turn the preserve bad. Ideally, all lids, stoppers and corks should be new, but if you are using old ones ensure they are in good condition without any corrosion, perished rubber seals, or ill-fitting stoppers.

1 To Clean Jars and Bottles: wash them in plenty of hot soapy water using a bottle brush to get into the crevices at the base and around the neck of the container. Rinse well in clean water and dry thoroughly. Do the same for the lids and stoppers. Alternatively use a dishwasher.

2 To Sterilize: a solution of Campden sterilizing tablets and water is best for bottles and corks. Make up and use the solution following the instructions on the packet.

3 Pour the solution into the containers through a funnel, leave for the amount of time specified on the packet, then pour out. Refrigerated syrups, cordials and juices will keep for 4 weeks, but sterilizing with water sterilizing tablets will extend their storage to 1 year.

Melting Chocolate

Working with chocolate can be tricky but these instructions are guaranteed fool-proof.

1 Always use fresh chocolate to ensure a good result. Break the chocolate into small pieces and place in a large, dry, clean bowl over a saucepan of hand-hot water.

2 Ensure that the base of the bowl does not touch the water and there are no spaces between the bowl and the rim of the saucepan which might cause steam and condensation to get into the chocolate, rendering it thick and unusable.

3 Do not beat the chocolate, but stir occasionally while it is melting. Don't try to hurry the process: the chocolate temperature should never exceed 100–110°F, otherwise when it eventually sets, the surface will be dull and covered in streaks.

4 Leave the bowl over hand-hot water during use, unless you want the chocolate to become thicker. Wipe the base of the bowl to remove any condensation.

Sweet Ingredients

Almonds
Almonds may be used blanched or with the skin intact. Blanched almonds, with the skins removed, have a sweet flavor and are ideal for cakes. Almonds with the skin intact are ideal for sweets, and delicious coated in chocolate or caramel.

Angelica
Green angelica stems preserved in sugar are used for cake decorating.

Chocolate
Chocolate in all its many forms is a firm favorite at Christmastime. Milk chocolate has a softer texture and sweeter flavor than plain chocolate. Plain chocolate, with its strong, rich flavor is ideal for melting and cooking. White chocolate is a product made with cocoa butter, which imparts a sweet, delicate flavor without the strong cocoa taste.

milk chocolate

plain chocolate

Cinnamon
Cinnamon may be used ground, or as a whole 'stick'. Cinnamon sticks impart a wonderful flavor to oils, vinegars and drinks.

Cloves
Cloves are full of flavor and are a delicious addition to spiced vinegars.

Crystalized ginger
This is preserved ginger root, coated in sugar. Its pungent flavor and crunchy outer layer makes it a good addition to home-made chocolates and candies.

Dates
Fresh or dried, dates are used in cakes, cookies, home-made chocolates and preserves.

Dried fruit
Mixed dried fruit is a blend of raisins, currants, orange and lemon peel and cherries, essential for Christmas cakes and puddings. Dried fruits are very nutritious, and have a very concentrated flavor.

Glacé fruit
Almost any fruit may be preserved in sugar syrup, and the colorful results make beautiful decorations. These can be fairly expensive to buy, but are very simple to make at home.

Hazelnuts
Hazelnuts may be used chopped in praline or cake mixtures, or finely ground.

Mace
Mace is the dried outer skin of the nutmeg, most often used ground. It has a milder flavor than nutmeg.

Nutmeg
Nutmeg can be bought whole, or as a powder. Freshly grated nutmeg has a wonderful flavor and aroma, and will impart a more powerful taste than the powdered form.

Pecan nuts
These nuts are similar to walnuts, but have a milder flavor. They make wonderful eating straight out of the shells, or may be bought as halves, or pieces for decoration and cooking.

Walnuts
Walnuts may be purchased in their shells, as walnut halves (ideal for decoration) or chopped for cake mixtures.

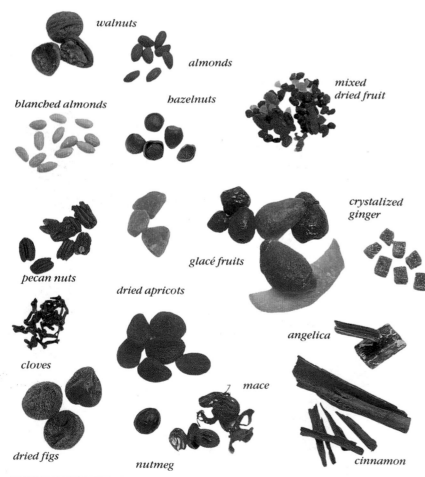

walnuts

almonds

blanched almonds

hazelnuts

mixed dried fruit

crystalized ginger

pecan nuts

glacé fruits

dried apricots

cloves

angelica

dried figs

mace

nutmeg

cinnamon

Fresh Fruit

Apples
So many varieties are available at Christmastime, and all have their own characteristics – soft or crisp flesh, red, green or golden skins. Choose firm apples for glacé fruits.

Apricots
Choose firm, ripe apricots for the best color and flavor.

Cherries
Purchase when in season, and use for glacé fruits or fruits in liqueurs. They are available at Christmastime, but are expensive.

Chinese gooseberries
Chinese gooseberries have a paper thin husk which should be peeled back before eating.

Clementines
These are available most of the year and may be used for glacé fruits, preserves or flavoring brandy.

Cranberries
These jewel-bright fruits are a colorful Christmas addition, available fresh at Christmastime, or frozen.

Grapes
A lovely addition to a Christmas fruit bowl.

peaches

apricots

apples

Available red, green or black, with or without seeds.

Kumquats
These tiny orange fruits have a citrus flavor. They may be used for glacé fruits, or making liqueurs, with the skin intact.

Lemons
Buy small lemons with fine skins for the best juice.

Limes
Small limes with smooth, bright green skins have the best flavor.

Lychees
A Christmas treat; choose pink-skinned fruits with sweet white flesh.

Paw paw
An exotic fruit, increasingly available in good supermarkets. Paw paws have a sweet pink flesh. Discard the seeds and skin, and use for glacé fruits or fruits in liqueurs.

Peaches
Peaches are best purchased in the summer, when they are in peak condition. They may sometimes be available at Christmastime – but at a cost. Ensure they are not bruised or damaged when buying. Use for fruits in liqueurs.

Pears
Many varieties of pear are

available. Make chutney when they are plentiful.

Plums
These are available all year round, but it is best to make use of indigenous varieties when in season.

Star fruit
These exotic fruits are available all the year round in good supermarkets. They are excellent preserved in liqueurs or used as glacé fruits.

Strawberries
Make the most of strawberries when in season, and bottle or use for preserves.

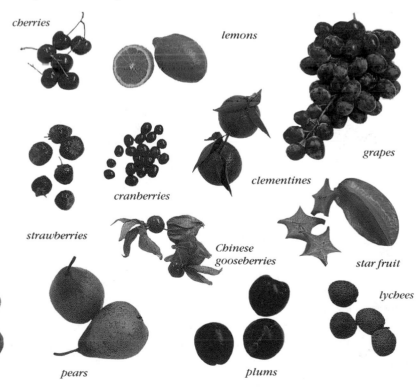

cherries
lemons
grapes
cranberries
clementines
strawberries
Chinese gooseberries
star fruit
lychees
limes
pears
plums

Savory Ingredients

The following are just some of the ingredients used in the savory recipes in this book. Always use the freshest, best quality ingredients available.

Anchovies
These have a very concentrated flavor, and are a great addition to fish pâtés.

Bacon slices
Bacon or fat back keeps home-made pâtés moist and full of flavor.

Bay leaves
Bay leaves are available fresh or dried. They make a flavorful and decorative addition to bottled oils and vinegars.

Basil
A wonderfully aromatic herb used in oils and vinegars.

Celery
Celery imparts a great texture to vegetable chutneys and pickles.

Cheshire cheese
A mild cheese with a crumbly texture, use in potted spreads.

Chilies
Fresh chilies must be handled carefully. Remove the seeds from chilies to lessen their impact.

Dill
Dill is particularly suited to fish dishes. The leaf may be finely chopped and added to pâtés.

Garlic
Fresh heads of garlic divide into single cloves, which may be used crushed or whole.

Ginger root
Use the fresh root grated in sweet or savory dishes.

Jarlsburg cheese
A Norwegian cheese similar to Emmenthal, good for cheese spreads.

Kippers
Kippers are smoked herrings; use in fish pâtés.

Maytag blue cheese
This red, blue-veined cheese is a good addition to cheese spreads.

Olives
Olives, both black and green, impart a strong flavor and color to pâtés and spreads.

Onions
Use large onions for chutneys and small onions pickled whole.

Parmesan cheese
A strongly flavored cheese from Italy. Use freshly grated for the best flavor.

Peppers
Red, yellow and green peppers may be preserved in oil, or used in pepper jelly.

Peppercorns
Green and black peppercorns impart flavor and decoration to oils and vinegars. Pink peppercorns are so-called because of their appearance, but they are not true peppercorns.

Rosemary
Use rosemary sparingly in meat dishes, or add to oils and vinegars.

Sage
Sage is available throughout the year. Use in herbed vinegars and flavored butters.

Salmon
Fresh salmon fillet may be used in pâtés and spreads.

Thyme
Thyme may be added to oils and vinegars, or peppers preserved in oil.

Tomatoes
Cherry tomatoes have the best flavor; larger tomatoes are good for cooking.

onions

basil

thyme

white peppercorns

k peppercorns

green peppercorns

bay leaves

ginger

dill

celery

anchovies

olives

kipper

peppers

sage

bacon slices

salmon

chilies

rosemary

Jarlsburg cheese

Parmesan cheese

tomatoes

garlic

Maytag blue cheese

Cheshire cheese

PRESENTATION IDEAS

All of the recipes in this book have been devised to be given as gifts, although they are so delicious you are sure to want to keep a batch yourself. There are many ways of packaging your gifts; the following are just a few ideas.

Marzipan fruits

Marzipan fruits look so delightful it's a shame to hide them away.

1 Choose a transparent container to show the fruits to best effect. This one is very simple in design, but you may wish to choose a more elaborate, glass container. Carefully position the fruits inside the container.

2 Finish with a co-ordinating ribbon or decoration, secured to the lid with double-sided tape.

Christmas cakes

These little cakes make ideal gifts. Prettily packaged they are the very essence of Christmas.

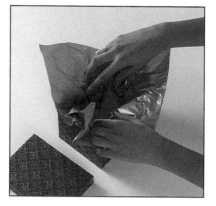 

1 For the container, a simple cardboard box covered in decorative paper was used. Line this with tissue paper in a festive color.

2 Carefully place the cake in the box, and cover with the remaining tissue paper. Please note, this packaging is purely decorative, and will not protect the cake if you are planning to send it long distances or in the mail.

Potted spreads and butters

Spreads and flavored butters are enchanting packed in little jars. Sterilize the container as explained earlier, pack with the chosen spread and decorate as follows.

Cookies and candies

If your gift will be given, and eaten, relatively quickly, and the contents do not need to be stored in an airtight container, then a pretty box lined with tissue paper may be the answer.

1 Decorate the top with ribbon curls in suitable colors (you may want to reflect the colors of the contents of the jars). Fix the ribbon curls in place with double-sided tape.

2 If you wish to present several assorted jars, pack them in a bag made of decorative wrapping paper.

1 Line your chosen container with 3–4 sheets of co-ordinating tissue paper. After positioning the first piece, lay the others on top, alternating the corners to fill the spaces. Crumpled tissue paper has a charm all its own. You may wish to crumple it first, then lightly smooth out.

2 Carefully place the contents inside the box, and fold excess tissue over the top for extra security.

Gift Wrappings

The emphasis on attractive gift wrappings has increased considerably in recent years. It is relatively simple to make small gifts at home and package them beautifully. Personalized gifts are as much a joy to give as receive, and will mean so much more.

There are many stores that specialize in gift wrapping materials. Papers, ribbons, different types of boxes, containers, labels and cards are all available. When making your own Christmas gifts, look out for unusual accessories with which to enhance the packaging of the fruits of your labors.

Boxes
These make wonderful containers for chocolates, candies, cakes or cookies. You will find many different designs, colors and sizes in stationers, paper specialists or large stores.

Fabrics
Choose fabrics printed with Christmas designs to make a simple drawstring bag or stocking shape as a container for a small gift. Cover the tops of preserves with a circle of fabric over the cellophane discs and cover boxes with bright fabrics using a clear fabric adhesive. You can also add ribbons or cut-out shapes.

Gift bags
These are especially useful for packing awkwardly shaped gifts such as pots of preserves or bottles. They come in a variety of sizes and often have a matching gift label attached.

Gift cards and tags
These are often available to co-ordinate with your chosen paper, box or container. You can easily make your own tags by sticking your chosen paper onto a plain piece of card before making a hole in the corner and adding a ribbon.

Glass bottles
There is now an extensive range of recycled glass containers in all sizes, suitable for bottling drinks, flavored oils and herbed vinegars. Many are available complete with their own air-tight stoppers or corks.

Glass jars
Assorted sizes of glass jars with screw-topped lids are invaluable for jams, jellies, savory butters and spreads. Found mostly in kitchen departments or stores, some jars come in wonderful shapes and have corks to seal the tops.

Ribbons
The choice is overwhelming; even the simplest ribbons can transform a gift more than any other packaging.

Small dishes
The choice is quite daunting and is limited only by how much you are willing to pay. Choose from rustic pottery dishes which are fun to receive, or plain white china presented in brightly colored wrapping paper. For a very special gift, choose a fine porcelain dish and place it in a box tied with co-ordinating ribbon.

Tins
These are often sold to store pens and pencils but make excellent air-tight containers for cookies, candies or small cakes, and can be found in many large stores, kitchen stores and stationers.

Right: *Bags and baskets, cards, and tags, ribbons and wrappings of all kinds can be used to enhance your home-made gifts.*

Chocolate Boxes

These tiny chocolate boxes make the perfect containers for handmade chocolates or candies. Use white or milk chocolate with dark trimmings to vary the theme.

Makes 4

INGREDIENTS
8 squares plain, or milk chocolate, melted
2 squares white chocolate

DECORATION
handmade chocolates or candies, to fill
2 yd ribbon, ½ in wide

milk chocolate

plain chocolate

white chocolate

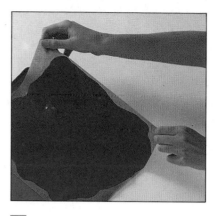

2 Pour all but 1 tbsp of the chocolate over the parchment paper and quickly spread to the edges using a metal spatula. Pick up 2 corners of the paper and drop; do this several times on each side to level the surface of the chocolate.

1 Line a large cookie sheet with parchment paper. Remove the bowl of melted chocolate from the heat and wipe the condensation off the base of the bowl.

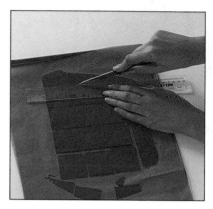

3 Leave the chocolate until almost set but still pliable. Place a clean piece of parchment paper on the surface, invert the chocolate sheet and peel the paper away from the back of the chocolate. Using a ruler and a scalpel or sharp knife, measure and cut the chocolate sheet into 2 in squares to form the sides of the boxes. Measure and cut out 2¼ in squares for the lids and bases of each of the boxes.

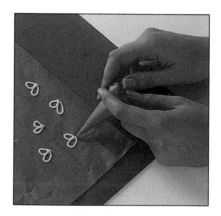

4 To assemble the boxes, paint a little of the remaining melted chocolate along the top edges of a chocolate square using a fine brush. Place the side pieces in position one at a time, brushing the side edges to join the 4 squares together to form a box. Leave to set. Repeat to make the remaining 3 boxes.

5 Melt the white chocolate and spoon into a waxed paper piping bag. Fold down the top and snip off the point. Pipe 20 chocolate loops onto a sheet of parchment paper and leave them to set.

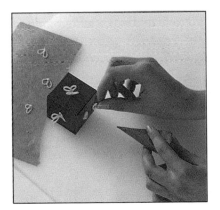

6 Decorate the sides of the boxes with chocolate loops, each secured with a bead of white chocolate. Alternatively, wrap a ribbon carefully around each box and tie a bow, having filled the boxes with chocolates or candies. Pack into gift boxes.

Fruit Fondant Chocolates

These chocolates are simple to make using pre-formed plastic molds, yet look very professional. Fruit fondant is available from sugarcraft stores and comes in a variety of flavors including coffee and nut. Try a mixture of flavors using a small quantity of each, or use just a single flavor.

Makes 24

INGREDIENTS
8 squares plain, milk or white
    chocolate
1 cup real fruit liquid fondant
3–4 tsp cooled boiled water

DECORATION
1 tbsp melted plain, milk or white
    chocolate

 milk chocolate

plain chocolate

white chocolate

1 Melt the chocolate. Use a piece of cotton wool to polish the insides of the chocolate molds, ensuring that they are spotlessly clean. Fill up the shapes in one plastic tray to the top, leave for a few seconds, then invert the tray over the bowl of melted chocolate allowing the excess chocolate to fall back into the bowl. Sit the tray on the work surface and draw a metal spatula across the top to remove the excess chocolate and to neaten the edges. Chill until set. Repeat to fill the remaining trays.

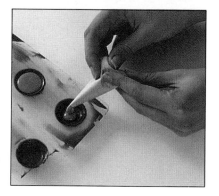

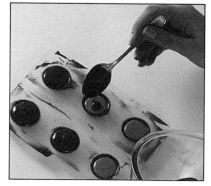

2 Sift the fruit fondant mixture into a bowl. Gradually stir in enough water to give it the consistency of thick cream. Place the fondant in a waxed paper piping bag, fold down the top and snip off the end. Fill each chocolate case almost to the top by piping in the fondant. Leave for 30 minutes or until a skin has formed on the surface of the fondant.

3 Spoon the remaining melted chocolate over the fondant to fill each mold level with the top. Chill until the chocolate has set hard. Invert the tray and press out the chocolates one by one. Place the melted chocolate of a contrasting color into a waxed paper piping bag, fold down the top, snip off the point and pipe lines across the top of each chocolate. Allow to set, then pack into pretty boxes and tie with ribbon.

Chocolate Truffles

These are popular with almost everybody; simply use different combinations of chocolate and flavorings to make your favorites.

Makes 60

INGREDIENTS
4 squares plain chocolate
4 squares milk chocolate
6 squares white chocolate
¾ cup heavy cream

FLAVORINGS
2 tbsp dark rum
2 tbsp Tia Maria
2 tbsp apricot brandy

COATINGS
3 tbsp coarsely grated plain chocolate
3 tbsp coarsely grated milk chocolate
3 tbsp coarsely grated white chocolate

milk chocolate

plain chocolate

white chocolate

I Melt each type of chocolate in a separate bowl. Place the cream in a small saucepan and heat gently until hot but not boiling. Allow to cool. Stir ⅓ of the cream into each of the bowls and blend evenly. Add the rum to the plain chocolate and whisk until the mixture becomes lighter in color. Whisk the Tia Maria into the milk chocolate and lastly whisk the apricot brandy into the white chocolate.

2 Allow the 3 mixtures to thicken, giving them an occasional stir, until they are thick enough to divide into equal spoonfuls. Line 3 cookie sheets with parchment paper. Place about 20 teaspoons of each flavored chocolate mixture, well spaced apart, onto the 3 cookie sheets and chill until firm enough to roll into small balls.

3 Place each of the grated chocolates into separate dishes. Shape the plain chocolate truffles into neat balls and roll in grated plain chocolate to coat evenly. Repeat with the milk chocolate truffles and grated milk chocolate and the white chocolate truffles and grated white chocolate. Chill the truffles until firm, then arrange neatly in boxes, bags or tins and tie with festive ribbon.

Chocolate Yule Log

This makes a delicious alternative to Christmas cake and is a real treat for chocolate lovers. Use the quantities below to make 4 individual logs if you are giving them as gifts.

Makes 1 large or 4 small logs

INGREDIENTS
3 eggs
5 tbsp superfine sugar, plus extra for sprinkling
¾ cup self-rising flour
1 tbsp cocoa powder

CHOCOLATE CREAM
5 tbsp superfine sugar
5 tbsp water
3 egg yolks
¾ cup unsalted butter
3 squares plain chocolate, melted

DECORATION
3 oz marzipan
green and red food colorings
confectioners' sugar and cocoa powder, to dust

eggs

plain chocolate

marzipan decorations

1 Preheat the oven to 375°F. Lightly grease a 13 × 9 in jelly roll pan and line with parchment paper. Place the eggs and sugar in a heatproof bowl over a saucepan of simmering water. Whisk the mixture until thick and pale, then remove the bowl from the saucepan. Continue to whisk until cool and thick, so that when the whisk is lifted it leaves a trail on the surface of the mixture.

2 Sift the flour and cocoa over the surface of the mixture and use a plastic scraper to fold in carefully until all the flour has been incorporated. Pour the mixture into the pan, tilt to level the mixture and bake in the oven for 18–20 minutes or until the cake springs back when lightly pressed in the center.

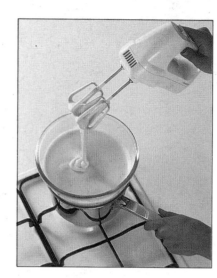

3 Place a piece of parchment paper onto a work surface and sprinkle with superfine sugar. Invert the sponge onto the paper and carefully remove the lining paper. Using a sharp knife, trim off all the edges and loosely roll up the sponge cake, including the paper, into a neat roll. Start from the long edge if you are making individual rolls or the short edge if you are making one large roll.

4 To make the chocolate cream, place the sugar and water into a saucepan. Heat gently until the sugar has dissolved, stirring occasionally. Boil rapidly to thread stage, 225°F on a sugar thermometer, or press a drop of syrup between 2 teaspoons; when pulled apart a thread should form. Place the egg yolks in a bowl; whisking well, gradually pour in the syrup. Whisk until the mixture is thick and pale. Leave to cool. Beat the butter until light and fluffy and gradually beat in the egg mixture until thick and fluffy. Fold in the melted chocolate.

5 Unroll the cake roll or rolls and remove the paper. Spread with half the chocolate cream and re-roll neatly. Spread the outside with the remaining chocolate cream and mark the surface with a metal spatula to make it look like 'bark'. Chill to set the icing.

6 Color ⅓ of the marzipan green and a tiny piece bright red with the food colorings. Roll out the green marzipan thinly and cut out 12 leaves using a holly leaf cutter. Mold lots of tiny berries from the red marzipan and 6 tiny toadstools from the plain marzipan. Decorate the chocolate log or logs with holly leaves, berries and toadstools. Dust with confectioners' sugar and cocoa powder.

Chocolate Christmas Cakes

This recipe may also be made as one 8 in square cake but 4 individual cakes look even more tempting and may be packed into pretty boxes.

Makes 4

INGREDIENTS
2½ cups self-rising flour
1 tbsp baking powder
¼ cup cocoa powder
1 cup 2 tbsp superfine sugar
⅔ cup sunflower oil
1½ cups water

ICING AND DECORATION
6 in square silver cake boards
6 tbsp Apricot Glaze (see
    Introduction)
2¼ lb marzipan
2 lb chocolate fondant
red, yellow and green food colorings
2 yd red ribbon
2 yd green ribbon

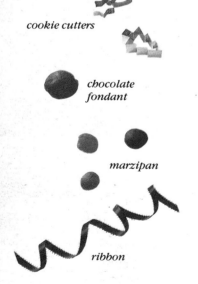

cookie cutters

chocolate
fondant

marzipan

ribbon

1 Preheat the oven to 325°F. Grease an 8 in square cake pan and line with waxed paper. Sift the flour, baking powder, cocoa powder and sugar into a mixing bowl.

2 Add the oil and water and mix together with a wooden spoon, beating until smooth and glossy. Pour into the prepared pan and bake in the oven for about 1 hour or until the cake springs back when pressed in the center.

3 Cool the cake in the pan for 15 minutes, then turn out, remove the paper and invert onto a wire rack. When completely cold, cut into 4 equal pieces, place each on a separate cake board and brush with Apricot Glaze.

4 Divide the marzipan into 4 equal pieces and roll out a piece large enough to cover one cake. Place over the cake, press neatly into shape and trim off the excess marzipan at the base of the board. Knead the trimmings together and repeat to cover the remaining 3 cakes.

5 Divide the chocolate fondant into 4 pieces and repeat the process, rolling out each piece thinly to cover each cake. Color the remaining marzipan ⅓ red, ⅓ yellow and ⅓ green with the food colorings. Thinly roll out each piece and cut into ½ in strips.

6 Lay alternate strips together and cut out 4 shapes using cookie cutters. Arrange the shapes on top of each cake. Measure and fit the red and green ribbons around each cake and tie a bow. Pack into pretty boxes, tie with ribbons and label.

Festive Gingerbread

These brightly decorated gingerbread cookies are fun to make and may be used as edible Christmas tree decorations.

Makes 20

INGREDIENTS
2 tbsp corn syrup
1 tbsp black molasses
¼ cup light brown sugar
2 tbsp butter
1½ cups flour
¾ tsp baking soda
½ tsp ground cinnamon
1½ tsp ground ginger
1 egg yolk

ICING AND DECORATION
½ quantity Royal Icing (see
   Introduction)
red, yellow and green food colorings
brightly colored ribbons

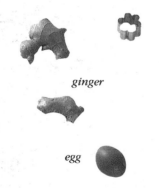

cookie cutters

ginger

egg

1 Preheat the oven to 375°F. Line several cookie sheets with parchment paper. Place the syrup, molasses, sugar and butter into a saucepan. Heat gently, stirring occasionally, until the butter has melted.

2 Sift the flour, baking soda, cinnamon and ginger into a bowl. Using a wooden spoon stir in the molasses mixture and the egg yolk and mix to a soft dough. Knead on a lightly floured surface until smooth.

3 Roll out the dough thinly and using a selection of festive cutters, stamp out as many shapes as possible, kneading and re-rolling the dough as necessary. Arrange the shapes well spaced apart on the cookie sheets. Make a hole in the top of each shape using a drinking straw if you wish to use the cookies as hanging decorations.

4 Bake in the oven for 15–20 minutes or until risen and golden and leave to cool on the cookie sheets before transferring to a wire rack using a metal spatula.

5 Divide the Royal Icing into 4 and color ¼ red, ¼ yellow and ¼ green using the food colorings. Make 4 waxed paper piping bags and fill each one with the different colored icings. Fold down the tops and snip off the points.

6 Pipe lines, dots, and zigzags on the gingerbread cookies using the colored icings. Leave to dry. Thread ribbons through the holes in the cookies.

Festive Shortbread

Light, crisp shortbread looks so professional when shaped in a mold, although you could also shape it by hand.

Makes 2 large or 8 individual shortbreads

INGREDIENTS
¾ cup plain flour
¼ cup cornstarch
¼ cup superfine sugar
½ cup unsalted butter

flour

sugar

butter

1 Preheat the oven to 325°F. Lightly flour the mold and line a cookie sheet with parchment paper. Sift the flour, cornstarch and sugar into a mixing bowl. Cut the butter into pieces and rub into the flour mixture until it binds together and you can knead it into a soft dough.

2 Place the dough into the mold and press to fit neatly. Invert the mold onto the cookie sheet and tap firmly to release the dough shape. Bake in the oven for 35–40 minutes or until pale golden.

3 Sprinkle the top of the shortbread with a little sugar and cool on the cookie sheet. Wrap in cellophane paper or place in a box tied with ribbon.

Christmas Tree Cookies

These cookies make an appealing gift. They look wonderful hung on a Christmas tree or in front of a window to catch the light.

Makes 12

INGREDIENTS
1½ cups plain flour
5 tbsp butter
3 tbsp superfine sugar
1 egg white
2 tbsp orange juice
8 oz colored fruit candies

DECORATION
colored ribbons

orange

egg

cookie cutter

candies

1 Preheat the oven to 350°F. Line 2 cookie sheets with parchment paper. Sift the flour into a mixing bowl. Cut the butter into pieces and rub into the flour until the mixture resembles fine breadcrumbs. Stir in the sugar, egg white and enough orange juice to form a soft dough. Knead on a lightly floured surface until smooth.

2 Roll out thinly and stamp out as many shapes as possible using a Christmas tree cutter. Transfer the shapes to the lined cookie sheets well spaced apart. Knead the trimmings together. Using a ½ in round cutter or the end of a plain meringue piping nozzle, stamp out and remove 6 rounds from each tree shape. Cut each candy into 3 and place a piece in each hole. Make a small hole at the top of each tree to thread through the ribbon.

3 Bake in the oven for 15–20 minutes, until the cookies are slightly gold in color and the candies have melted and filled the holes. Cool on the cookie sheets. Repeat until you have used up the remaining cookie dough and candies. Thread short lengths of ribbon through the holes so that you can hang up the cookies.

Gingerbread House

This gingerbread house makes a memorable family gift, especially if filled with lots of little gifts and surprises.

Makes 1

INGREDIENTS
6 tbsp corn syrup
2 tbsp black molasses
⅓ cup light brown sugar
5 tbsp butter
4 cups flour
1 tbsp ground ginger
1 tbsp baking soda
2 egg yolks
8 oz barley sugar candies

ICING AND DECORATION
1 quantity Royal Icing (see Introduction)
10 in square silver cake board

black molasses

cookie cutters

barley sugar candies

eggs

corn syrup

1 Preheat the oven to 375°F. Line several cookie sheets with parchment paper. Cut out the templates. Place the syrup, molasses, sugar and butter in a saucepan and heat gently, stirring occasionally until melted.

2 Sift the flour, ginger and baking soda into a bowl. Add the egg yolks and pour in the molasses mixture, stirring with a wooden spoon to form a soft dough. Knead on a lightly floured surface until smooth and place in a polythene bag. Cut off ⅓ of the dough and roll out thinly.

3 Place the template for the end walls at one end and cut neatly round the shape using a sharp knife. Repeat to cut another end wall. Place on the cookie sheet. Using a 1 in round cutter, stamp out 1 round window for each piece. Cut a door shape on each end wall, using the square cutter, then rounding off the tops. Place a candy in each of the windows and bake in the oven for 8–10 minutes until the candy has filled the frame and the gingerbread is golden brown. Cool on the cookie sheet.

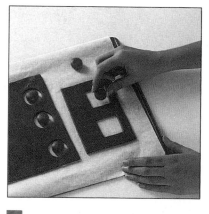

4 Repeat the above instructions using the remaining dough for the 2 side walls and the 2 roof pieces. Using a 1 in square cutter, stamp out 2 window shapes for each wall piece. Using a 1 in round cutter, stamp out 3 round windows for each roof piece. Place candies in the openings and bake as before.

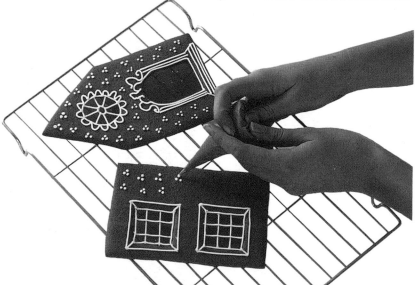

5 Make the Royal Icing. Place some of the icing in a waxed paper piping bag fitted with a No. 2 plain writing nozzle. Pipe lines, loops and circles around the windows, doors and on the walls and roof to decorate. Pipe beads of icing in groups of 3 all over the remaining spaces and leave flat to dry.

TEMPLATES FOR THE GINGERBREAD HOUSE

1 For the side wall, measure and cut out a rectangle 6 in × 4 in from stiff cardboard.

2 For the pitch of the roof, measure and cut out a rectangle 7 in × 4 in. Measure 4 in up each long side and mark these points. Mark a center point at the top of the short edge. Draw a line from each of the side points to the top point. Cut out.

3 For the roof, measure and cut out a rectangle 8 in × 6 in from stiff cardboard.

6 To assemble the house, pipe a line of icing on the side edges of the walls and side pieces. Stick them together to form a box shape on the cake board. Pipe a line of icing following the pitch of the roof on both end pieces and along the top of the 2 roof pieces. Press gently in position and support the underneath of each roof while the icing sets. Pipe the finishing touches to the roof and base of the house. Dust the cake board with confectioners' sugar to look like snow. Wrap ribbon around the edges of the board.

Cheese Biscuits

These crispy cheese biscuits are irresistible, and will disappear in moments. Try using different cheeses sprinkled with a variety of seeds to give alternative flavors.

Makes about 80

INGREDIENTS
1 cup flour
½ tsp salt
½ tsp cayenne pepper
½ tsp powdered mustard
½ cup butter
½ cup grated Cheddar
½ cup grated Gruyère
1 egg white, beaten
1 tbsp sesame seeds

sesame seeds

cayenne pepper

egg

Cheddar

Gruyère

powdered mustard

1 Preheat the oven to 425°F. Line several cookie sheets with parchment paper. Sift the flour, salt, cayenne pepper and mustard into a mixing bowl. Cut the butter into pieces and rub into the flour mixture until it begins to cling together.

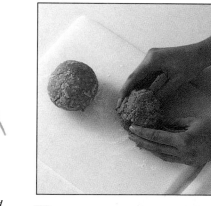

2 Divide the mixture in half, add the Cheddar to 1 half and the Gruyère to the other. Using a fork, work each mixture into a soft dough and knead on a floured surface until smooth.

3 Roll out both pieces of dough very thinly and cut into 1 in squares. Transfer to the lined cookie sheets. Brush the squares with beaten egg white, sprinkle with sesame seeds and bake in the oven for 5–6 minutes or until slightly puffed up and pale gold in color. Cool on the cookie sheets, then carefully remove with a metal spatula. Repeat the process until you have used up all the biscuit dough. Pack into tins or boxes and tie with ribbon.

Cocktail Biscuits

Tiny savory biscuits are always a welcome treat. Try using different flavors and shapes and pack the biscuits into brightly colored tins.

Makes about 80

INGREDIENTS
3 cups flour
½ tsp salt
½ tsp black pepper
1 tsp whole grain mustard
¾ cup butter
½ cup grated Cheddar
1 egg, beaten

FLAVORINGS
1 tsp chopped nuts
2 tsp dill seeds
2 tsp curry paste
2 tsp chili sauce

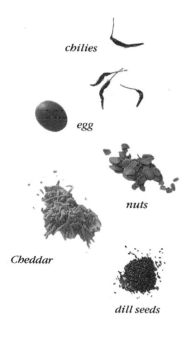

chilies

egg

nuts

Cheddar

dill seeds

1 Preheat the oven to 400°F. Line several cookie sheets with parchment paper. Sift the flour into a mixing bowl and add the salt, pepper and mustard. Cut the butter into pieces and rub into the flour mixture until it resembles fine breadcrumbs. Use a fork to stir in the cheese and egg, and mix together to form a soft dough. Knead lightly on a floured surface and cut into 4 equal pieces.

2 Knead chopped nuts into one piece, dill seeds into another piece and curry paste and chili sauce into each of the remaining pieces. Wrap each piece of flavored dough in plastic wrap and leave to chill in the fridge for at least an hour. Remove from the plastic wrap and roll out one piece at a time.

3 Using a heart-shaped cutter, stamp out about 20 shapes from the curry-flavored dough and use a club-shaped cutter to cut out the chili-flavored dough. Arrange the shapes well spaced apart on the cookie sheets and bake in the oven for 6–8 minutes or until slightly puffed up and pale gold in color. Cool on wire racks. Repeat with remaining flavored dough using spade- and diamond-shaped cutters. Knead any trimmings together, re-roll and stamp out and bake as above.

Striped Cookies

These cookies may be made in different flavors and colors and look wonderful tied in bundles or packed into boxes. Eat them with ice cream or light desserts.

Makes 25

INGREDIENTS
1 square white chocolate, melted
red and green food coloring dusts
2 egg whites
⅓ cup superfine sugar
½ cup flour
4 tbsp unsalted butter, melted

egg

icing bag

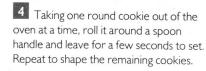

white chocolate

1 Preheat the oven to 375°F. Line 2 cookie sheets with parchment paper. Divide the melted chocolate in 2 and add a little food coloring dust to each half to color the chocolate red and green. Using 2 waxed paper piping bags, fill with each color chocolate and fold down the tops. Snip off the points.

2 Place the egg whites in a bowl and whisk until stiff. Add the sugar gradually, whisking well after each addition, to make a thick meringue. Add the flour and melted butter and whisk until smooth.

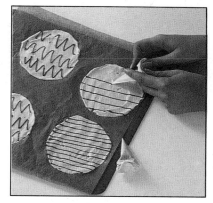

3 Drop 4 separate teaspoonsfuls of mixture onto the cookie sheets and spread into thin rounds. Pipe lines or zigzags of green and red chocolate over each round. Bake in the oven for 3–4 minutes or until pale golden in color. Loosen the rounds with a metal spatula and return to the oven for a few seconds to soften. Have 2 or 3 lightly oiled wooden spoon handles at hand.

4 Taking one round cookie out of the oven at a time, roll it around a spoon handle and leave for a few seconds to set. Repeat to shape the remaining cookies.

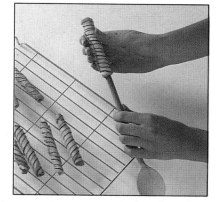

5 When the cookies are set, slip them off the spoon handles onto a wire rack. Repeat with the remaining mixture and the red and green chocolate until all the mixture has been used, baking only one sheet of cookies at a time. If the cookies are too hard to shape, simply return them to the oven for a few seconds to soften.

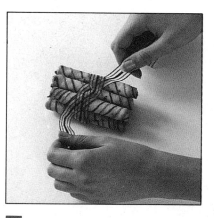

6 When the cookies are cold, tie them together with colored ribbon and pack into boxes, tins or glass jars.

Mini Iced Christmas Cakes

A personal Christmas cake makes an extra special gift.
Try improvising with your own designs, decorations
and color schemes

Makes 1 large or 4 individual cakes

INGREDIENTS
1½ cups mixed dried fruit
¼ cup glacé cherries, sliced
½ cup slivered almonds
grated rind of ½ lemon
1 tbsp brandy
1 cup flour
½ tsp ground cinnamon
⅓ cup ground almonds
½ cup unsalted butter, softened
½ cup dark brown sugar
½ tbsp black molasses
2 eggs

ICING AND DECORATION
4 in square cake boards
4 tbsp Apricot Glaze (see
   Introduction)
1½ lb white marzipan
2 lb ready-to-roll icing
red and green food colorings

I Prepare a 6 in square cake pan. Place
the mixed dried fruit, cherries, almonds,
lemon rind and brandy into a large mixing
bowl. Stir until thoroughly blended, cover
with plastic wrap and leave for I hour or
overnight.

2 Preheat the oven to 300°F. Sift the
flour and mixed spice into another bowl,
add the ground almonds, butter, sugar,
molasses and eggs. Mix together with a
wooden spoon and beat for 2–3 minutes
until smooth and glossy. Alternatively use
a food mixer or processor for I minute.
Fold the fruit into the cake mixture until
evenly blended. Place the mixture in the
prepared pan, level the top and make a
slight dent in the center.

3 Bake the cake in the center of the
oven for 2¼–2½ hours or until a skewer
inserted into the center of the cake
comes out clean. Leave the cake to cool
in the pan. Spoon over a little extra
brandy if desired. Remove the cake from
the pan and wrap in foil until required.

 *lemon*

 glacé cherries

almonds

 marzipan

4 Remove the lining paper and cut the
cake into 4 square pieces. Place each cake
on a small cake board and brush evenly
with Apricot Glaze. Cut the marzipan into
4 pieces and roll out a piece large enough
to cover one cake. Place over the cake,
smooth over the top and sides and trim
off the excess marzipan at the base.
Repeat to cover the remaining 3 cakes.

5 Cut the ready-to-roll icing into 5 pieces, roll 4 pieces out thinly to cover each cake, smoothing the tops and sides and trimming off the excess icing at the bases. Knead the trimmings together with the remaining piece of icing and cut into 2 pieces. Color one piece red and the other piece green using the food colorings. Roll out ½ of the red icing into a 10 × 6 in oblong.

6 Cut the icing into ¼ in strips and place diagonally across the cake working from corner to corner. Trim the strips at the base of the cake. Brush the ends of the strips with a little water and press onto the cake. Make a few loops of icing and place on top of the cake. Repeat to decorate the remaining cakes with green and finally red and green strips of icing. Pack into boxes when dry.

Mini Black Buns

Black bun is a traditional Scottish recipe with a very rich fruit cake mixture cooked inside a bun dough. This variation uses marzipan in place of the dough.

Makes 4

INGREDIENTS
4 tbsp butter, melted, plus extra for brushing
1 cup mixed dried fruit
¼ cup glacé cherries, chopped
½ cup chopped almonds
2 tsp grated lemon rind
2 tbsp superfine sugar
1 tbsp whisky
½ cup flour
1 tsp ground cinnamon
1 egg, beaten

DECORATION
2 tbsp Apricot Glaze (see Introduction)
1 lb white marzipan
purple and green food colorings

marzipan

lemon

dried fruit

almonds

glacé cherries

1 Preheat the oven to 300°F. Cut out 6 in squares of waxed paper and 4 squares of foil. Place the waxed paper squares on top of the foil squares and brush with a little melted butter.

2 Place the dried fruit, cherries, almonds, lemon rind, sugar, whisky, sifted flour and cinnamon into a large mixing bowl. Using a wooden spoon, stir until well mixed. Add the melted butter and egg and beat together until well blended.

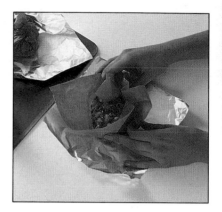

3 Divide the mixture between the 4 paper and foil squares, draw up the edges to the center and twist to mold the mixture into rounds. Place on a cookie sheet and bake in the oven for 45 minutes or until the mixture feels firm when touched. Remove the foil and bake for a further 15 minutes. Open the paper and cool on a wire rack.

4 Remove the paper and brush each cake with Apricot Glaze. Cut off ¼ of the marzipan for decoration and put to one side. Cut the remainder into 4 pieces.

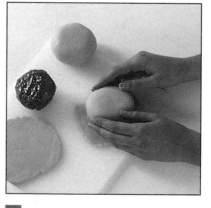

5 Roll out each piece thinly and cover the cakes, tucking the joins underneath. Roll each cake in the palms of your hands to make them into round shapes. Prepare a hot broiler and place the cakes onto a cookie sheet lined with foil.

6 Broil the cakes until the marzipan is evenly browned. Leave until cold. Color ½ of the remaining marzipan purple and ½ green with food colorings. Cut out 4 purple thistle shapes, green leaves and stems and arrange them on top of each cake, moistening with a little water to stick. Wrap in cellophane and place into small cake boxes.

Individual Fruit Cakes

These delicious little fruit cakes may be topped with almonds or covered with glacé fruits.

Makes 3

INGREDIENTS
1 cup raisins
1 cup currants
1 cup golden raisins
¼ cup glacé cherries, sliced
¾ cup orange and lemon peel
grated rind of 1 orange
2¾ cups flour
½ tsp baking powder
1 tsp ground cinnamon
1 cup unsalted butter, softened
1 cup superfine sugar
5 eggs

TOPPING
½ cup whole blanched almonds
¼ cup glacé cherries, halved
½ cup glacé fruits, sliced
3 tbsp Apricot Glaze (see Introduction)

orange

glacé cherries

almonds

peel

egg

glacé fruits

1 Preheat the oven to 300°F. Prepare 5 in round cake pans. Place all the fruit and the orange rind into a large mixing bowl. Mix together until evenly blended. In another bowl sift the flour, baking powder and cinnamon. Add the butter, sugar and eggs. Mix together with a wooden spoon and beat for 2–3 minutes until smooth and glossy. Alternatively use a food mixer or processor for 1 minute.

2 Add the mixed fruit to the cake mixture and fold in using a plastic scraper until well blended. Divide the cake mixture between the 3 pans and level the tops. Arrange the almonds in circles over the top of one cake, the glacé cherries over the second cake and the mixed glacé fruits over the last one. Bake in the oven for approximately 2–2½ hours or until a skewer inserted into the center of the cakes comes out clean.

3 Leave the cakes in their pans until completely cold. Turn out, remove the paper and brush the tops with Apricot Glaze. Leave to set, then wrap in cellophane paper or plastic wrap and place in pretty boxes.

Spiced Christmas Cake

This light cake mixture is flavored with spices and fruit. It can be served with a dusting of confectioners' sugar and decorated with holly leaves.

Makes 1

INGREDIENTS
1 cup butter, plus extra for greasing
    mold
1 tbsp fresh white breadcrumbs
1 cup superfine sugar
¼ cup water
3 eggs, separated
2 cups self-rising flour
1½ tsp ground cinnamon
2 tbsp chopped angelica
2 tbsp orange and lemon peel
¼ cup glacé cherries, chopped
½ cup walnuts, chopped
confectioners' sugar, to dust

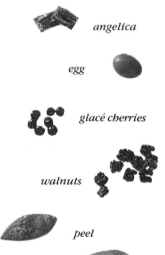

angelica

egg

glacé cherries

walnuts

peel

1 Preheat the oven to 350°F. Brush an 8 in, 2½ pint fluted ring mold with melted butter and coat with breadcrumbs, shaking out any excess.

2 Place the butter, sugar and water into a saucepan. Heat gently, stirring occasionally, until melted. Boil for 3 minutes until syrupy, then allow to cool. Place the egg whites in a clean bowl, whisk until stiff. Sift the flour and cinnamon into a bowl, add the angelica, orange and lemon peel, cherries and walnuts and stir well to mix. Add the egg yolks.

3 Pour the cooled mixture into the bowl and beat together with a wooden spoon to form a soft batter. Gradually fold in the egg whites using a plastic spatula until the mixture is evenly blended. Pour into the prepared mold and bake for 50–60 minutes or until the cake springs back when pressed in the center. Turn out and cool on a wire rack. Dust thickly with sugar and decorate with a sprig of holly.

Novelty Christmas Cakes

These individual cakes can be packed in their own little boxes to make unusual gifts for children.

Makes 2

INGREDIENTS
1 cup self-rising flour
1 tsp baking powder
1 tbsp cocoa powder
½ cup superfine sugar
½ cup soft margarine
2 eggs

DECORATION
3 tbsp Apricot Glaze (see
  Introduction)
2 × 6 in thin round cake boards
12 oz ready-to-roll icing
350 g/12 oz white marzipan
red, black, green, yellow and brown
  food colorings
white and red glitter flakes

marzipan

eggs

glitter flakes

1 Preheat the oven to 325°F. Grease and line the bases of 2 × 6 in round sandwich pans. Place all the cake ingredients into a large mixing bowl. Mix together with a wooden spoon and beat for 2–3 minutes until smooth and glossy.

2 Divide the mixture between the 2 pans, smooth the tops and bake in the oven for 20–25 minutes or until the cakes spring back when pressed in the center. Loosen the edges of the cakes and invert onto a wire rack. Remove the paper.

3 Brush both the cakes with Apricot Glaze and place on their cake boards. To make the clown cake, roll out ⅓ of the icing to a round large enough to cover one cake. Place the icing over the cake, smooth the surface and trim off the excess at the base. Mold 2 ears from the trimmings and press into position.

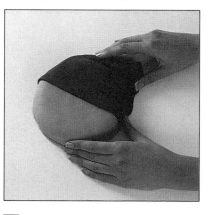

5 To make the Santa Claus cake, color the remaining marzipan skin tone using a tiny amount of brown coloring and roll out thinly to cover ⅔ of the second cake. Trim to fit. Roll out ¾ of the red marzipan thinly and cover the remaining ⅓ of the cake to make the hat. Gather the excess together at one side for the hat. Mold a nose and mouth from the remaining red marzipan.

4 Color ⅓ of the marzipan red and shape a mouth and nose; reserve the remainder. Color a small piece of marzipan black and roll out thin lengths to outline the mouth and make the eyebrows and 2 crosses for the eyes.

Color another small piece green for the ruffle. Color another small piece yellow and grate coarsely to make the hair. Stick in position with Apricot Glaze and sprinkle with the white glitter flakes.

6 Coarsely grate the remaining white icing and use to trim the hat and to shape the beard, moustache and eyebrows. Gently press a small ball of grated icing together to make a bobble for the hat. Shape 2 black eyes and press in position. Sprinkle red glitter flakes onto the hat to give a sparkle. Pack each cake into a small box with a lid and write a name tag.

Round Christmas Pudding

A round Christmas pudding makes a wonderful novelty gift. Special molds are available from supply stores in large and small sizes.

Makes 1 large or 2 small puddings

INGREDIENTS
4 tbsp butter, melted, plus extra for
　brushing
1½ cups mixed dried fruit
1 cup dried mixed fruit salad,
　chopped
½ cup slivered almonds
1 small carrot, coarsely grated
1 small apple, coarsely grated
grated rind and juice of 1 lemon
1 tbsp black molasses
6 tbsp dark beer
1 cup fresh white breadcrumbs
½ cup flour
1 tsp ground allspice
¼ cup dark brown sugar
1 egg

apple

carrot

egg

lemon

dried fruit

almonds

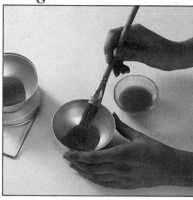

1 Lightly butter 5 in round Christmas pudding mold or 3 in molds, and place a disc of parchment paper in the base of each half. Have a saucepan ready into which the pudding mold will fit comfortably.

4 Spoon the mixture into both halves of the mold so they are evenly filled. At this stage insert silver coins or miniature keepsakes wrapped several times in waxed paper.

2 Place all the dried fruits, nuts, carrot and apple into a large mixing bowl. Mix everything together with a wooden spoon. Stir in the lemon rind and juice, molasses and beer until well blended. Cover with plastic wrap and leave in a cool place for a few hours or overnight.

5 Place the 2 halves of the mold together, stand on the base and clip firmly together to secure during cooking. Carefully place the mold into the saucepan. Half-fill the saucepan with boiling water, taking care that the water does not reach any higher than the join of the mold. Bring to a boil, cover and simmer very gently for 5–6 hours, being sure to replenish the saucepan with boiling water during the cooking time.

3 Add the breadcrumbs, sifted flour, allspice, sugar, butter and egg. Mix together until thoroughly blended.

6 Carefully remove half the mold and leave until the pudding is cold. Turn out, wrap in cellophane paper and tie with ribbon with a sprig of holly.

Flavored Vinegars

Flavored vinegars look extra special if you pour them into beautifully shaped bottles. Use fresh herbs and flowers, spices and soft fruits.

Makes 2½ cups of each flavor

INGREDIENTS
good quality red and white wine
   vinegar or cider vinegar

HERB VINEGAR
1 tbsp mixed peppercorns
2 lemon slices
4 garlic cloves
rosemary, thyme and tarragon sprigs

SPICE VINEGAR
1 tbsp allspice berries
2 mace blades
2 tsp star anise
2 cinnamon sticks
1 orange

FRUIT VINEGAR
3 cups raspberries
3 cups gooseberries
3 cups blackberries or elderberries

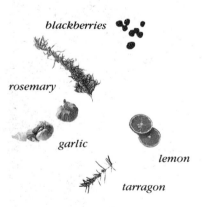

blackberries

rosemary

garlic

lemon

tarragon

1 Sterilize 2 bottles with corks or caps. To the first bottle add the peppercorns, lemon slices and garlic cloves. Place the herb sprigs together and trim the stems so they vary in length. Insert them into the bottle, placing the short ones in first.

2 Into the second bottle add the allspice berries, mace, star anise and cinnamon sticks. Cut 2 slices from the orange and insert into the bottle. Pare the rind from the remaining orange, taking care not to include any pith. Insert into the bottle.

3 Using white wine vinegar, fill the bottle containing the herbs up to the neck. Repeat to fill the bottle containing the spices with red wine vinegar. Cork or cap the bottles and store in a cool place.

4 Wash the raspberries, gooseberries and blackberries or elderberries separately and place into separate bowls. Crush with a wooden spoon.

5 Pour each fruit into a separate clean wide-necked jar and add 2½ cups of white wine vinegar. Cover and leave for 3–4 days in a cool place. Shake the jars occasionally to mix well.

6 Strain each fruit separately through a jelly bag or a muslin-lined sieve into a stainless steel saucepan and boil for 10 minutes. Pour into sterilized bottles or jars and seal with lids or tops with plastic coated linings. Use all vinegars within 6 months.

Fresh Fruit Preserve

The wonderfully fresh flavor of this fruit spread makes it a welcome gift. To vary the recipe, use a mixture of soft fruits, or other individual fruits such as strawberries or blackberries.

Makes 2 lb

INGREDIENTS
3½ cups raspberries
4 cups superfine sugar
2 tbsp lemon juice
½ cup liquid pectin

raspberries

lemon

1 Place the raspberries in a large bowl and lightly crush with a wooden spoon. Stir in the sugar. Leave for 1 hour at room temperature, giving the mixture an occasional stir to dissolve the sugar.

2 Sterilize several small jars or containers, and their lids if being used. Add the lemon juice and liquid pectin to the raspberries and stir until thoroughly blended.

3 Spoon the raspberry mixture into the jars, leaving a ½ in space at the top if the preserve is to be frozen. Cover the surface of each preserve with a waxed paper disc and cover with a lid or cellophane paper and an elastic band. Don't use a screw-topped lid if the preserve is to be frozen. Allow to cool, then label and freeze for up to 6 months, or refrigerate for up to 4 weeks.

Flavored Oils

Any good quality oils may be flavored with herbs, spices, peppers, olives or anchovies. They look attractive in the kitchen, as well as being ready flavored for use in cooking or salad dressings.

Makes 1¼ cups of each flavor

INGREDIENTS
olive, grapeseed or almond oil

HERB OIL
sage, thyme, oregano, tarragon and
    rosemary sprigs
1 bay leaf sprig

SPICED OIL
2 tbsp whole cloves
3 mace blades
1 tbsp cardamom pods
1 tbsp coriander seeds
3 dried chilies
1 bay leaf sprig
2 lime slices
2 cinnamon sticks

MEDITERRANEAN OIL
2 mini red peppers
3 black olives
3 green olives
3 anchovy fillets
1 bay leaf sprig
strip of lemon rind

1 Have ready 3 bottles and corks which have been sterilized and are completely dry inside. Place all the fresh herb sprigs together and trim to fit inside the first bottle. Insert the short lengths first and arrange them using a long skewer, adding them stem by stem.

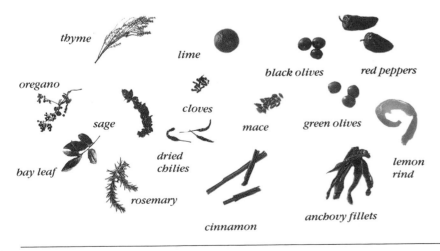

thyme
oregano
sage
bay leaf
rosemary
cloves
dried chilies
cinnamon
lime
black olives
mace
green olives
anchovy fillets
red peppers
lemon rind

2 Add the cloves, mace, cardamom pods, coriander seeds and chilies to the second bottle. Insert the bay leaf, lime slices and cinnamon sticks.

3 Grill the mini red peppers until they are tender, turning once. Add the olives, anchovies and peppers to the last bottle. Insert the bay leaf sprig and strip of lemon rind. Fill each bottle with the chosen oil and cork or cap. Label clearly and keep cool until required.

Red Pepper and Rosemary Jelly

This wonderful amber-colored jelly may be made with either red or yellow peppers and flavored with any full-flavored herbs. It is delicious with cold meat, poultry, fish or cheeses.

Makes 4 lb

INGREDIENTS
8 tomatoes, chopped
4 red peppers, seeded and chopped
2 red chilies, seeded and chopped
rosemary sprigs
1¼ cups water
1¼ cups red wine vinegar
½ tsp salt
5 cups granulated sugar with added pectin
1 cup liquid pectin

peppers

rosemary

tomatoes

chilies

1 Place the tomatoes, peppers, chilies, a few rosemary sprigs and the water into a stainless steel saucepan and bring to a boil. Cover and simmer for 1 hour or until the peppers are tender and pulpy.

2 Suspend a jelly bag and place a bowl underneath. Sterilize the jelly bag by pouring through boiling water. Discard the water and replace the bowl.

3 Pour the contents of the saucepan slowly into the jelly bag. Allow the juices to drip through slowly for several hours but do not squeeze the bag or the jelly will become cloudy. Sterilize the jars and lids required.

4 Place the juice into a clean saucepan with the vinegar, salt and sugar. Discard the pulp in the jelly bag. Heat gently, stirring occasionally, until the sugar has dissolved. Boil rapidly for 3 minutes.

5 Remove the saucepan from the heat and stir in the liquid pectin. Skim the surface with a piece of paper towelling to remove any foam.

6 Pour the liquid into the sterilized jars and add a sprig of rosemary to each jar. Place a waxed disc onto the surface of each and seal with a lid or cellophane paper and a rubber band. Allow to cool, then label and decorate with ribbons.

Crab Apple and Lavender Jelly

This fragrant, clear jelly looks even prettier with a sprig of fresh lavender suspended in the jar. Try using other fruits such as apples, quince or rosehips.

Makes about 2 lb

INGREDIENTS
5 cups crab apples
7½ cups water
lavender stems
4 cups granulated sugar

lavender

crab apples

1 Cut the crab apples into chunks and place in a preserving pan with water and 2 stems of lavender. Bring to a boil and cover the pan with a piece of foil or a lid and simmer very gently for 1 hour, giving the mixture an occasional stir, until the fruit is pulpy.

4 Discard the pulp and measure the quantity of juice in the bowl. To each 2½ cups of juice add 2 cups of sugar and pour into a clean pan. Sterilize the jars and lids required.

2 Suspend a jelly bag and place a bowl underneath. Sterilize the jelly bag by pouring through some boiling water. Discard the water and replace the bowl.

3 Pour the contents of the saucepan slowly into the jelly bag. Allow the juice to drip slowly through for several hours but do not squeeze the bag or the jelly will become cloudy.

5 Heat the juice gently, stirring occasionally, until the sugar has dissolved. Bring to a boil and boil rapidly for about 8–10 minutes until setting point has been reached. When tested, the temperature should be 221°F. If you don't have a sugar thermometer, put a small amount of jelly on a cold plate and allow to cool. The surface should wrinkle when you push your finger through the jelly. If not yet set, continue to boil and then re-test.

6 Remove the pan from the heat and use a slotted spoon to remove any froth from the surface. Carefully pour the jelly into a pitcher, then fill the warm sterilized jars. Dip the lavender quickly into boiling water and insert a stem into each jar. Cover with a disc of waxed paper and with cellophane paper and a rubber band. Label when cold.

Peppers in Olive Oil

The wonderful flavor and color of these peppers will add a Mediterranean theme to festive foods. Bottle the peppers separately or mix the colors together for a gift that tastes as good as it looks.

Makes enough to fill 3 × 1 lb jars

INGREDIENTS
3 red peppers
3 yellow peppers
3 green peppers
1¼ cups olive oil
½ tsp salt
½ tsp freshly ground black pepper
3 thyme sprigs

peppers

thyme

1 Prepare a hot broiler or preheat the oven to 400°F. Put the whole peppers on a broiling pan or onto a cookie sheet. Place under the broiler or in the oven and cook for about 10 minutes until the skins are charred and blistered all over. Turn frequently during cooking.

2 Allow the peppers to cool for at least 5 minutes, then peel off the skins. Remove the cores, seeds and stalks. Slice each of the peppers thinly, keeping each color separate, and place each into a separate dish.

3 Pour ⅓ of the olive oil over each of the peppers. Sprinkle with salt and pepper and add a sprig of thyme to each dish. Stir to blend well. Sterilize 3 jars and lids and fill each with a mixture of peppers, or keep them separate. Top up each jar with the oil. Screw firmly down and label.

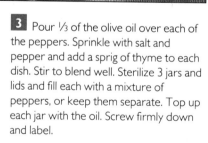

Christmas Chutney

This chutney makes the perfect accompaniment to cold meats, pâtés and cheese. It has a sweet but spicy flavor and the fruits may be changed for quince, greengage or rhubarb.

Makes 4 lb

INGREDIENTS
9 plums, pitted
16 pears, peeled and cored
2 apples, peeled and cored
4 stalks celery
1 lb onions, sliced
1 lb tomatoes, skinned
½ cup raisins
1 tbsp grated fresh ginger root
2 tbsp pickling spice
3¾ cups cider vinegar
2 cups granulated sugar

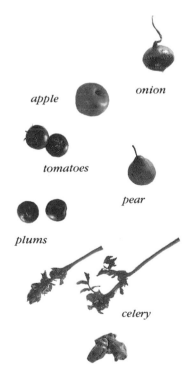

apple

onion

tomatoes

pear

plums

celery

ginger

1 Chop the plums, pears, apples, celery and onions and cut the tomatoes into quarters. Place all these ingredients with the raisins and ginger into a very large saucepan.

2 Place the pickling spice into a piece of muslin and tie with string to secure. Add to the saucepan with half the vinegar and bring to the boil, giving the mixture an occasional stir. Cook for about 2 hours.

3 Meanwhile sterilize the jars and lids. When all the ingredients are tender, stir in the remaining vinegar and the sugar. Boil until thick, remove the bag of spices and fill each jar with chutney. Cover with a wax paper disc and plastic lid and label when cold.

Fruits in Liqueurs

These eye-catching fruits in liqueurs are best made when the fruits are plentiful, cheap and in season. Choose from apricots, clementines, kumquats, cherries, raspberries, peaches, plums or seedless grapes and team them with rum, brandy, kirsch or Cointreau just to name a few.

Makes 1 lb

INGREDIENTS
3 cups fresh fruit
1 cup granulated sugar
⅔ cup liqueur or spirits

apricots

clementines

kumquats

Chinese gooseberries

1 Wash the fruit, halve and pit apricots, plums or peaches. Peel back and remove the husk from Chinese gooseberries, hull strawberries or raspberries, and prick kumquats, cherries or grapes all over with a toothpick. Pare the rind from clementines using a sharp knife, taking care not to include any white pith.

2 Place ½ cup of the sugar and 1¼ cups of water into a saucepan. Heat gently, stirring occasionally, until the sugar has dissolved. Bring to a boil.

3 Add the fruit to the syrup and simmer gently for 1–2 minutes until the fruit is just tender, but the skins are intact and the fruits are whole.

4 Carefully remove the fruit using a slotted spoon and arrange neatly into the warmed sterilized jars. Add the remaining sugar to the syrup in the pan and stir until dissolved.

5 Boil the syrup rapidly until it reaches 230°F or the thread stage. Test by pressing a small amount of syrup between 2 teaspoons; when they are pulled apart, a thread should form. Allow to cool.

6 Measure the cooled syrup, then add an equal quantity of liqueur or spirit. Mix until blended. Pour over the fruit in the jars until covered. Seal each jar with a screw or clip top, label and keep for up to 4 months.

Anchovy Spread

This delicious spread has a concentrated flavor and is best served with plain toast.

Makes 2¹/₂ cups

INGREDIENTS

2 × 2 oz cans anchovy fillets in olive
  oil
4 garlic cloves, crushed
2 egg yolks
2 tbsp red wine vinegar
1¼ cups olive oil
¼ tsp freshly ground black pepper
2 tbsp chopped fresh basil or thyme

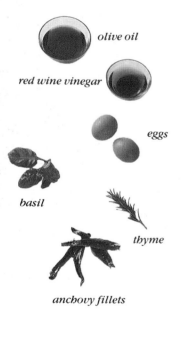

olive oil

red wine vinegar

eggs

basil

thyme

anchovy fillets

1 Drain the oil from the anchovies and reserve. Place the anchovies and garlic in a food processor. Process until smooth. Add the egg yolks and vinegar, and process until the egg and vinegar have been absorbed by the anchovies.

2 Measure out the oil into a measuring cup and add the reserved anchovy oil. Set the food processor to a low speed and add the oil drop by drop to the anchovy mixture until it is thick and smooth.

3 Add some freshly ground black pepper and fresh herbs, and blend until smooth. Spoon the mixture into small sterilized jars, cover and label. Store in the fridge.

Smoked Salmon Pâté

This luxury pâté makes a fine gift for a special person. Pack the pâté in a pretty dish to give as part of the gift. Store in the fridge.

Makes enough to fill 4 small ramekin dishes

INGREDIENTS
12 oz fresh salmon fillet
¼ tsp salt
½ tsp freshly ground black pepper
1 tbsp chopped fresh dill, plus sprigs
　to garnish
4 slices smoked salmon
½ cup cottage or cream cheese
5 tbsp unsalted butter
1 cup fresh white breadcrumbs
1 tsp lemon juice
2 tbsp Madeira

lemon

dill

salmon fillet

smoked salmon

1 Preheat the oven to 375°F. Put the salmon fillet on a large piece of waxed paper placed on top of a sheet of foil. Sprinkle with salt, pepper and dill. Seal the foil and place on a cookie sheet. Cook in the oven for 10 minutes or until just tender. Leave until cold and remove the skin, saving any of the juices.

2 Cut out 4 pieces of smoked salmon to fit the bases of the 4 individual dishes. Cut out 4 strips to fit around the inside edges of each dish. Cover and chill.

3 Place the cooked salmon, its juices, the cheese, butter, breadcrumbs, lemon juice and Madeira into a food processor. Process until smooth. Divide the mixture between the dishes and press it down to fill each dish evenly. Cover the top with another piece of smoked salmon and decorate with a sprig of dill. Cover with plastic wrap and chill.

Smoked Kipper Spread

This wonderful spread will be a welcome change of flavor at Christmas. Spread it on hot toast for an instant snack.

Makes enough to fill 4 small ramekin dishes

INGREDIENTS
½ cup unsalted butter
12 oz kipper fillets, cooked
grated rind and juice of 1 lime
2 tsp tomato paste
2 tbsp whisky
1 cup wholewheat breadcrumbs
½ tsp freshly ground black pepper

TO GARNISH
4 bay leaves
4 black olives, halved

black olives

bay leaves

lime

kipper fillets

tomato paste

1 Melt 3 oz of the butter and place with the kippers into a food processor. Process until smooth. Add the lime rind and juice, tomato paste, whisky, breadcrumbs and pepper. Process again, until smooth.

2 Fill 4 individual ramekins with the spread and press down well leaving a ½ in space at the top. Cover and chill.

3 Melt the remaining butter and cool. Pour over each pot to fill to the top. Garnish with bay and olives. Chill until set, then cover with plastic wrap.

Potted Cheese Rarebit

An instant 'cheese on toast' in a pot. Try using Gruyère cheese instead of the Cheddar as a variation. You may wish to serve it with a sprinkling of Worcestershire sauce or a bit of chopped anchovy.

Makes 1 ½ lb

INGREDIENTS
4 tbsp butter
1 tbsp herbed French mustard
½ tsp freshly ground black pepper
½ cup ale or cider
1 lb mature Cheddar, grated

Cheddar

black pepper

French mustard

1 Place the butter, mustard, pepper and ale or cider into a saucepan. Heat gently, stirring occasionally, until boiling.

2 Add the cheese, take off the heat and stir until the cheese has melted and the mixture is creamy.

3 Pour the mixture into sterilized pots, cover and leave until cold. Chill to set, then label.

Farmhouse Pâté

This pâté is full of flavor and can be cut into slices for easy serving. You can make the pâté in 4 individual dishes, or make 1 pâté in a 1 lb container.

Makes 1 lb

INGREDIENTS
8 slices bacon
2 chicken breasts
8 oz chicken livers
1 onion, chopped
1 garlic clove, crushed
½ tsp salt
½ tsp freshly ground black pepper
1 tsp chopped anchovy fillet
1 tsp ground mace
1 tbsp chopped fresh oregano
1 cup fresh white breadcrumbs
1 egg
2 tbsp brandy
⅔ cup chicken stock
2 tsp gelatin

TO GARNISH
strips of pimento and black olives

onion

egg

chicken breast

chicken livers

bacon

1 Preheat the oven to 325°F. Press the bacon slices flat with a knife to stretch them. Line the base and sides of each dish with bacon and neatly trim the edges.

2 Place the chicken breasts and livers, onion and garlic into a food processor. Process until smooth. Add the salt, pepper, chopped anchovy, mace, oregano, breadcrumbs, egg and brandy. Process until smooth.

3 Divide the mixture between the dishes and fill to the top. Cover each with double thickness foil and stand the dishes in a roasting pan. Add enough hot water to come halfway up the side of the dishes.

4 Bake in the center of the oven for 1 hour or until firm to touch. Release the foil to allow the steam to escape. Place a weight on the top of each dish to flatten the surface until cool.

5 Pour the juices from each dish into a measuring cup and make up to ⅔ cup with chicken stock. Heat in a small saucepan until boiling. Blend the gelatin with 2 tbsp water and pour into the hot stock, stir until dissolved. Allow to cool thoroughly.

6 When the pâté is cold, arrange strips of pimento and black olives on the top of each. Spoon the cold gelatin mixture over the top of each and chill until set. Cover each with plastic wrap. Store in the fridge until required.

Savory Butters

This selection of 8 tiny pots of unusual flavored butters can be used as garnishes for meat, fish and vegetables, as a topping for canapés or as a tasty addition to sauces.

Makes about ¼ cup of each flavor

INGREDIENTS
2 cups unsalted butter
2 tbsp Stilton
3 anchovy fillets
1 tsp curry paste
1 garlic clove, crushed
2 tsp finely chopped fresh tarragon
1 tbsp prepared horseradish
1 tbsp chopped fresh parsley
1 tsp grated lime rind
¼ tsp chili sauce

Stilton

lime

tarragon

garlic

parsley

anchovy fillets

1 Place the butter in a food processor. Process until light and fluffy. Divide the butter into 8 portions.

2 Crumble the Stilton and mix together with a portion of butter. Pound the anchovies to a paste in a pestle and mortar and mix with the second portion of butter. Stir the curry paste into the third, and the crushed garlic into the fourth portion.

3 Stir the tarragon into the fifth portion and the horseradish into the sixth portion. Into the seventh portion add the parsley and the lime rind, and to the last portion add the chili sauce. Pack each flavored butter into a tiny sterilized jar and label clearly. Store in the fridge.

Brandy Butter

No Christmas pudding is complete without brandy butter and it is simple to make. Pack into pretty jars or china containers tied with festive ribbon.

Makes 1 1/2 lb

INGREDIENTS
1 cup unsalted butter
1 cup superfine sugar
1/2 cup brandy

DECORATION
marzipan holly leaves and berries

brandy

superfine sugar

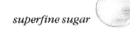
marzipan decorations

butter

1 Bring the butter to room temperature before using, then place in a bowl or a food processor. Beat with a wooden spoon until light and smooth, or process until smooth.

2 Add the sugar and beat or process until the mixture is light and fluffy. Continue to beat or process adding the brandy a little at a time, beating or processing well after each addition. Do not add the brandy too quickly or the mixture will curdle.

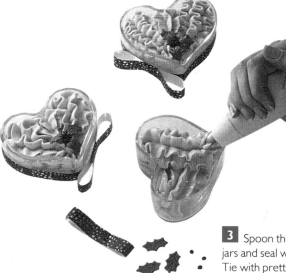

3 Spoon the brandy butter into clean jars and seal with clean lids. Label and chill. Tie with pretty ribbon and a gift label. To decorate, pipe into small dishes using a fluted nozzle and decorate with small marzipan holly leaves and berries.

Christmas Cards

These decorative sugar greeting cards make ideal gifts. The Modeling Paste may be cut to any size and a variety of cutters or piping nozzles used to create the design. Double the quantity of Modeling Paste to make more cards.

Makes 4

INGREDIENTS
½ quantity Modeling Paste
gold, green, red and purple food colorings
brown, red, green and purple food coloring pens
½ yd each of ⅛ in wide brown, red, green and purple ribbon

food coloring pens

cookie cutters

modeling paste

1 Make the Modeling Paste. Color the paste a pale cream color using a few drops of gold food coloring and cut into 4 pieces. Taking a piece at a time, roll out until the paste is ⅛ in thick. Using a 3½ in fluted oval cutter, stamp out 2 oval shapes. Stamp out a small oval from the center of one shape using a 2 in plain oval cutter.

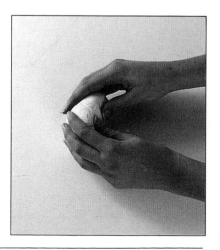

2 Using a No. 1 plain writing nozzle, carefully stamp out tiny holes in each fluted shape around the edge of each oval. Make 2 holes ½ in apart in the center of the left-hand side on both shapes so they match together when the ribbon is threaded through. Place the oval shape with the cut-out center on a board. Using a small heart-shaped cutter, stamp out a series of hearts around the cut-out section. Use the plain nozzle to cut holes between the heart shapes.

MODELING PASTE

INGREDIENTS
1½ cups confectioners' sugar
1 tbsp gum tragacanth
1 tsp liquid glucose
1–2 tbsp water

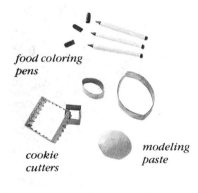

1 Sift the icing sugar and gum tragacanth into a bowl. Make a well in the center and add the liquid glucose and water. Mix together with your fingers to form a soft paste. Dust a surface with confectioners' sugar and knead the sugarpaste until smooth, and free from cracks.

2 Place in a plastic bag or wrap in plastic wrap and seal well to exclude all the air. Leave for 2 hours before use, then re-knead and use small pieces at a time, leaving the remaining Modeling Paste well sealed. Use a little margarine instead of sugar when kneading, rolling out or molding the paste, to prevent it from becoming dry and brittle.

3 Leave the pieces to dry on a piece of foam sponge. Repeat to make 3 more cards in different shapes and sizes. When the cards are dry, arrange the 2 pieces of each card with the cut centers on top. Mark a series of dots within the cut-out center, matching each food coloring pen to the ribbon color, and write the name or greeting inside. Alternatively, cut out tiny holly leaves and berries and apply to the front of the card. Thread the ribbon through the holes to secure the cards together. They will keep indefinitely if stored in a cool, dry place.

Sugar Boxes

These delightful boxes may be made in any size or shape you choose. Decorate them with a freehand design or apply cut out decorations if you prefer.

Makes 4

INGREDIENTS
1 quantity Modeling Paste
1 quantity Gum Glaze
green and red food coloring dusts or
    ready-blended food colorings

cutter

paintbrushes

food colorings

1 Measure around the outside of a plain round 3 in cutter with a length of string and cut it to size. Dust the outside of the cutter with cornstarch. Roll out a small piece of Modeling Paste thinly and cut to the length of the string and to the depth of the cutter. Gently ease the strip to fit inside the cutter so that the edges overlap, cutting away any excess paste. Brush the cut ends of the joins with a little Gum Glaze and press together to join neatly. Run a knife between the paste and the cutter to ensure the ring moves freely. Remove the cutter when the paste is firm.

2 Roll out another piece of paste thinly. Stamp out 2 rounds using the same cutter and place on a foam sponge. Mold a small knob for the lid, brush the underneath with Gum Glaze and press in position on the lid.

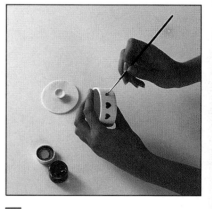

3 Brush the base edge of the box with Gum Glaze and place it in position on the round base. Repeat to make another 3 boxes. Leave all the pieces in a warm place to dry overnight. Using a fine pencil, draw a freehand design of holly leaves and berries, hearts, or your chosen design onto the side and lid of the box. Using food coloring dust mixed with a little Gum Glaze or ready-blended food colorings, and a fine paintbrush, paint one color at a time, cleaning the brush well before using each new color, until all the design has been painted. When dry, fill with a small gift or candies.

GUM GLAZE

INGREDIENTS
1 tbsp gum arabic
1 tbsp water

1 Gum Glaze is much more effective than egg white for sticking together sugar paste items. It dries very quickly and sets the sugar paste. Blend the gum arabic with the water using a small whisk and beat until smooth and free from lumps. Place in a tiny screw-topped jar or container.

Napkin Rings

These pretty rings may be used as a table decoration and taken home afterwards as a keepsake.

Makes 4

INGREDIENTS
1 quantity Modeling Paste
red, green, gold and silver glitter food coloring dusts
2 tbsp Royal Icing (see Introduction)

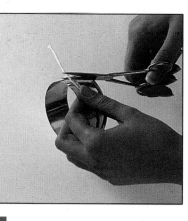

cookie cutter

Modeling Paste decorations

1 Make the Modeling Paste. Measure a piece of string to fit around the outside of a 3 in plain cutter and cut to size.

2 Roll out a small piece of Modeling Paste to the length of the string and measuring 1 in wide, and 1/8 in thickness. Using a knife, cut out the measured shape and round off both ends.

3 Brush the surface of the Modeling Paste with red glitter dust to color evenly. Place the strip of paste inside the cutter so the ends just meet. When the paste has set remove the cutter.

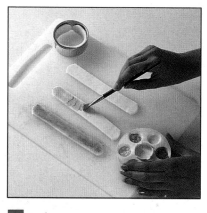

4 Color the remaining strips green, silver and gold, and make another 3 napkin ring shapes. Place all 4 rings on a foam sponge and leave in a warm dry place for 48 hours until completely dry and hard.

5 To make the decorations, use some Modeling Paste to form a selection of tiny fruits and vine leaves following the instructions for Marzipan Fruits. Color each fruit and leaf using the glitter dust and allow to dry. Using holly and ivy leaf cutters, make a selection of leaves and berries, rolling out the paste thinly and coloring with green and red glitter dusts. Mark the veins on the leaves with a knife and bend each leaf to dry over a wooden dowel or acrylic skewer.

6 Apply the holly, ivy leaves and berries to the red and green napkin rings, securing each piece with a little Royal Icing. Arrange the fruit and vine leaves on the gold and silver napkin rings, securing them with Royal Icing. Leave overnight to dry and pack into individual boxes.

Hanging Christmas Decorations

Decorations made from sugar Modeling Paste dry as hard as ceramic tiles. Many shapes and designs may be accomplished by imagination and flair. Ready-to-roll icing may be used instead of Modeling Paste but allow much longer for drying.

Makes 6

INGREDIENTS
1 quantity Modeling Paste or
    8 oz ready-to-roll icing or fondant
1 quantity Gum Glaze
red and green food colorings
1½ yd red ribbon, ½ in wide
3 yd green ribbon, ½ in wide

Modeling Paste

cookie cutters

ribbon

1 Make the Modeling Paste and Gum Glaze or use ready-to-roll icing or fondant instead. Color ⅓ of the paste a bright red and ⅔ a rich green using the red and green food colorings, and knead until evenly colored and smooth. Keep in a plastic bag.

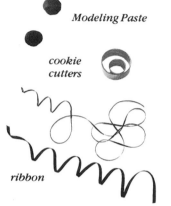

2 Using ½ of the green paste, roll out to a thickness of about ¼ in. Using a 3 in plain round pastry cutter, stamp out 3 rounds. Using a 2 in plain cutter, stamp out the center of each round to leave 3 rings. Take a small cocktail heart cutter and stamp out 3 heart shapes. Place all these cut-outs on a piece of foam sponge.

3 Brush the surface of one ring with Gum Glaze. Press some of the green paste through a garlic press, allowing the strands to fall evenly over the ring. Repeat to cover the remaining 2 rings. Roll out the red paste and using a 3 in heart-shaped cutter, stamp out 3 hearts and secure the small hearts in the center of each large heart using a little Gum Glaze. Make a hole in the top of each wreath and heart. Form lots of tiny berries and arrange at intervals on the wreath. Leave all pieces to dry hard, then thread ribbon through each.

Gold and Silver Christmas Bell Decorations

These are simply made by pressing sugar or Modeling Paste into a set of different sized bell-shaped molds. They can be colored, decorated or left plain.

Makes 6

INGREDIENTS
1 quantity Modeling Paste or 8 oz
  ready-to-roll icing or fondant
1 quantity Gum Glaze
cornstarch, to dust
1 tsp gin or vodka
gold and silver food coloring dusts
1½ yd gold ribbon, ⅛ in wide
1½ yd silver ribbon, ⅛ in wide

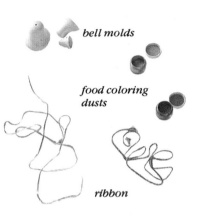

bell molds

food coloring dusts

ribbon

1 Make the Modeling Paste and Gum Glaze. Cut the paste into 6 even-sized pieces, returning 5 to the plastic bag. Lightly dust a work surface with cornstarch and shake a little into the inside of the largest bell mold.

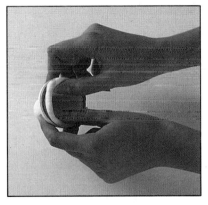

2 Gently ease the paste around the inside of a bell mold keeping the paste smooth. When the top end of the bell is smooth and a good shape, work down to the rim of the bell and trim off the excess with a knife. Pierce a hole in the top of the bell using a stainless steel needle. Repeat to make the medium- and small-sized bells, leave to dry. When the bells are hard, ease them out of the molds and repeat to make another set.

3 Using a fine paintbrush brush the outside of one bell with alcohol. Dust with gold food coloring dust to coat evenly. Repeat to color one set gold and one set silver. Cut each ribbon into 3 pieces. Mold 6 pea-shapes of paste for the 'clappers' and color 3 gold and 3 silver. Make a hole in the center of each, brush with Gum Glaze and insert the gold and silver ribbons. Thread the ribbon through each bell until the clapper is just above the rim. Press a small piece of paste, brushed with Gum Glaze, to the top of the bell to hold the ribbon in position, and tie the ribbon in a loop.

Candle Centerpiece

This arrangement of festive foliage and Christmas roses can be made in advance. Choose a brightly colored candle for the center.

Makes 1

INGREDIENTS
1 quantity Modeling Paste
1 quantity Gum Glaze
dark and light green and red food colorings
yellow and green food coloring dusts
2 tbsp Royal Icing (see Introduction)

Modeling Paste

food colorings

cookie cutters

1 Make the Modeling Paste and Gum Glaze. Keep well sealed in a plastic bag during use. Divide the modeling paste into 3 pieces. Color 1 piece dark green and 1 piece light green using the food colorings. Place in the plastic bag. Take a pea-sized piece from the remaining white paste and color it bright red for the holly berries. Seal well.

2 To make the rose: roll out a small piece of white paste on an acrylic board so thinly that you can almost see through it. Using a Christmas rose cutter, cut out 5 petal shapes. Soften the edges by using a bone tool on a flower mat or piece of foam sponge and make them slightly cup-shaped. Roll out a tiny piece of dark green paste and cut out a calyx and place on the flower mat or foam.

3 Brush the calyx with a little Gum Glaze and arrange the petals on it one at a time so that they overlap slightly, and stick them together with Gum Glaze. Position the flower over the hole in the flower mat or pierced hole if you are using foam sponge. Mold a tiny piece of white paste into a bead shape, brush with Gum Glaze and dip into yellow food coloring dust.

4 Place the yellow bead in the center of the rose and place the rose over a round cutter to support the petals while drying. Leave to dry in a warm place and repeat to make another 4 roses.

5 Roll out the light green paste. Using large and small-sized holly cutters, stamp out 8 large and 8 small holly leaves. Mark in the veins with a knife and bend over an acrylic skewer or wooden dowel to give each leaf a realistic shape. Roll out the

dark green paste and cut out 8 medium-sized ivy leaves. Leave to dry. Mold lots of tiny red berries. Brush the surface of each leaf with Gum Glaze and green food coloring dust to give them a gloss.

6 Knead the remaining green colored pastes together and roll into 2 × 10 in pencil thin lengths. Twist together to form a rope and join the ends together to make a circle. Place on a board. Arrange the Christmas roses, holly and ivy leaves around the ring and add a few berries. Secure each element with a little Royal Icing. Leave to set hard in a warm place.

Marzipan Fruits

These eye-catching and realistic fruits will make a perfect gift for lovers of marzipan.

Makes 1 lb

INGREDIENTS
1 lb white marzipan
yellow, green, red, orange and
  burgundy food coloring dusts
2 tbsp whole cloves

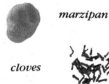

marzipan

cloves

food coloring dusts

1 Cover a cookie sheet with parchment paper. Cut the marzipan into quarters. Take 1 piece and cut it into 10 even-sized pieces. Place a little of each of the food coloring dusts into a palette, or place small amounts spaced apart on a plate. Cut ⅔ of the cloves into 2 pieces, making a stem and core end.

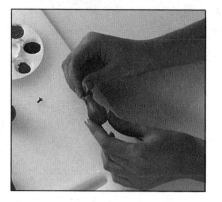

2 Taking the 10 pieces, shape each one into a neat ball. Dip 1 ball into the yellow food coloring dust and roll between the palms of the hands to color. Re-dip into the green coloring and re-roll to tint a greeny-yellow color. Using your forefinger, roll one end of the ball to make a pear shape. Press a clove stem into the top and a core end into the base. Repeat with the remaining 9 balls of marzipan. Place on the cookie sheet.

3 Cut another piece of the marzipan into 10 pieces and shape into balls. Dip each piece into green food coloring dust and roll in the palms to color evenly. Add a spot of red coloring dust and roll to blend the color. Using a ball tool or the end of a paintbrush, indent the top and base to make an apple shape. Insert a stem and core.

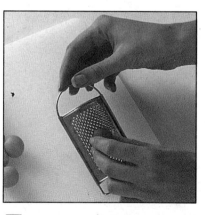

4 Repeat as above using another piece of the marzipan to make 10 orange colored balls. Roll each over the surface of a fine grater to give the texture of an orange skin. Press a clove core into the base of each.

5 Take the remaining piece of marzipan, reserve a small piece, and mold the rest into lots of tiny marzipan beads. Color them burgundy with the food coloring dust. Place a whole clove on the cookie sheet. Arrange a cluster of burgundy beads in the shape of a bunch of grapes. Repeat with the remaining burgundy beads of marzipan to make another 3 bunches of grapes.

6 Roll out the remaining tiny piece of marzipan thinly and brush with green food coloring dust. Using a small vine leaf cutter, cut out 8 leaves, mark the veins with a knife and place 2 on each bunch of grapes, bending to give a realistic appearance. When all the marzipan fruits are dry, pack into gift boxes.

Turkish Delight

Turkish Delight is always a favorite at Christmas, and this versatile recipe can be made in minutes. Try different flavors such as lemon, crème de menthe and orange and vary the colors accordingly.

Makes 1 lb

INGREDIENTS
2 cups granulated sugar
1¼ cups water
1 oz powdered gelatin
½ tsp cream of tartar
2 tbsp rose-water
pink food coloring
3 tbsp confectioners' sugar, sifted
1 tbsp cornstarch

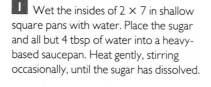

cream of tartar

gelatin

rose-water

sugar

food colorings

1 Wet the insides of 2 × 7 in shallow square pans with water. Place the sugar and all but 4 tbsp of water into a heavy-based saucepan. Heat gently, stirring occasionally, until the sugar has dissolved.

2 Blend the gelatin and remaining water in a small bowl and place over a saucepan of hot water. Stir occasionally until dissolved. Bring the sugar syrup to a boil and boil steadily for about 8 minutes or until the syrup registers 260°F on a sugar thermometer. Stir the cream of tartar into the gelatin, then pour into the boiling syrup and stir until well blended. Remove from the heat.

3 Add the rose-water and a few drops of pink food coloring to tint the mixture pale pink. Pour the mixture into the pans and allow to set for several hours or overnight. Dust a sheet of waxed paper with some of the sugar and cornstarch. Dip the base of the pan in hot water. Invert onto the paper. Cut into 1 in squares using an oiled knife. Toss in confectioners' sugar to coat evenly.

Orange, Mint and Coffee Meringues

These tiny, crisp meringues are flavored with orange, coffee and mint chocolate sticks and liqueurs. Pile into dry, air-tight glass jars or decorative tins.

Makes 90

INGREDIENTS
8 chocolate mint sticks
8 chocolate orange sticks
8 chocolate coffee sticks
½ tsp crème de menthe
½ tsp orange curaçao or Cointreau
½ tsp Tia Maria
3 egg whites
¾ cup superfine sugar
1 tsp cocoa powder

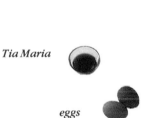

Tia Maria

eggs

crème de menthe

chocolate mint sticks

1 Preheat the oven to 225°F. Line 2–3 cookie sheets with parchment paper. Chop each flavor of chocolate stick separately and place each into separate bowls, retaining a teaspoonful of each flavor stick. Stir in the liquid flavorings to match the chocolate sticks.

2 Place the egg whites in a clean bowl and whisk until stiff. Gradually add the sugar, whisking well after each addition until thick. Add ⅓ of the meringue to each bowl and fold in gently using a clean plastic scraper until evenly blended.

3 Place about 30 teaspoons of each mixture onto the cookie sheets, well spaced apart. Sprinkle the top of each meringue with the reserved chopped chocolate sticks, matching the flavors. Bake in the oven for 1 hour or until crisp. Allow to cool and dust lightly with cocoa.

Creamy Fudge

A good selection of fudge always makes a welcome change from chocolates. Mix and match the flavors to make a gift-wrapped assortment.

Makes 2 lb

INGREDIENTS
4 tbsp unsalted butter, plus extra for greasing
2 cups granulated sugar
1¼ cups heavy cream
⅔ cup milk
3 tbsp water (this can be replaced with orange, apricot or cherry brandy, or strong coffee)

FLAVORINGS
1 cup plain or milk chocolate chips
1 cup chopped almonds, hazelnuts, walnuts or brazil nuts
½ cup chopped glacé cherries, dates or dried apricots

walnuts

almonds

glacé cherries

hazelnuts

plain chocolate chips

1 Butter a 8 in shallow square pan. Place the sugar, cream, butter, milk and water or other flavoring into a large heavy-based saucepan. Heat very gently, stirring occasionally using a long-handled wooden spoon, until all the sugar has completely dissolved.

2 Bring the mixture to a boil and boil steadily, stirring only occasionally to prevent the mixture from burning over the base of the saucepan. Boil until the fudge reaches just under soft ball stage, 230°F for a soft fudge.

3 If you are making chocolate flavored fudge, add the chocolate at this stage. Remove the saucepan from the heat and beat thoroughly until the mixture starts to thicken and become opaque.

4 Just before this consistency has been reached, add chopped nuts for a nutty fudge, or glacé cherries or dried fruit for a fruit-flavored fudge. Beat well until evenly blended.

5 Pour the fudge into the prepared pan, taking care as the mixture is exceedingly hot. Leave the mixture until cool and almost set. Using a sharp knife, mark the fudge into small squares and leave in the pan until quite firm.

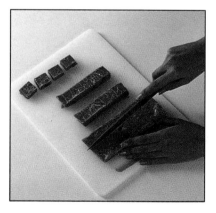

6 Turn the fudge out onto a board and invert. Using a long-bladed knife, cut into neat squares. You can dust some with confectioners' sugar and drizzle others with melted chocolate if desired.

Macaroons

These little macaroons can be served as petit-fours or with coffee. To make chocolate macaroons, replace the cornstarch with cocoa powder.

Makes 30

INGREDIENTS
½ cup ground almonds
¼ cup superfine sugar
1 tbsp cornstarch
¼–½ tsp almond extract
1 egg white, whisked
15 slivered almonds
4 glacé cherries, quartered
confectioners' sugar or cocoa, to dust

egg

glacé cherries

almonds

1 Preheat the oven to 325°F. Line 2 cookie sheets with parchment paper. Place the ground almonds, sugar, cornstarch and almond extract into a bowl and mix together well using a wooden spoon.

2 Stir in enough egg white to form a soft piping consistency. Place the mixture into a nylon piping bag fitted with a ½ in plain piping nozzle.

3 Pipe about 15 rounds of mixture onto each cookie sheet well spaced apart. Press a slivered almond onto half the macaroons and quartered glacé cherries onto the remainder. Bake in the oven for 10–15 minutes until firm to touch. Cool on the paper and dust with sugar or cocoa before removing from the paper.

Truffle Christmas Puddings

Truffles disguised as Christmas puddings are great fun to make and receive. Make any flavored truffle, and decorate them as you like.

Makes 20

INGREDIENTS
20 plain chocolate truffles
1 tbsp cocoa powder
1 tbsp confectioners' sugar
1 cup white chocolate chips, melted
2 oz white marzipan
green and red food colorings
yellow food coloring dust

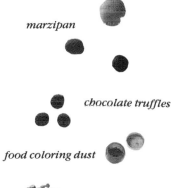

marzipan

chocolate truffles

food coloring dust

white chocolate chips

1 Make the truffles following the recipe on page 25. Sift the cocoa powder and sugar together and coat the truffles.

2 Spread ⅔ of the melted white chocolate over a piece of parchment paper. Pick up the corners and shake to level the surface. Using a 1 in daisy cutter, stamp out 20 rounds when the chocolate has just set. Place a truffle on the center of each daisy shape, secured with a little of the reserved melted chocolate. Leave to set.

3 Color ⅔ of the marzipan green and ⅓ red using the food colorings. Roll out the green thinly and stamp out 40 leaves using a tiny holly leaf cutter. Mark the veins with a knife. Mold lots of tiny red beads. Color the remaining white chocolate with yellow food coloring dust and place in a waxed paper piping bag. Fold down the top, cut off the point and pipe over the top of each truffle to resemble custard. Arrange the holly leaves and berries on the top. When set, arrange in gift boxes and tie with ribbon.

Marshmallows

These light and fragrant mouthfuls of pale pink mousse are flavored with rose-water. Try using orange-flower water as a contrast, and color the sweets with a hint of orange food coloring.

Makes 1¼ lb

INGREDIENTS
oil, for greasing
3 tbsp confectioners' sugar
3 tbsp cornstarch
¼ cup cold water
3 tbsp rose-water
1 oz powdered gelatin
pink food coloring
2 cups granulated sugar
2 level tbsp liquid glucose
1 cup boiling water
2 egg whites

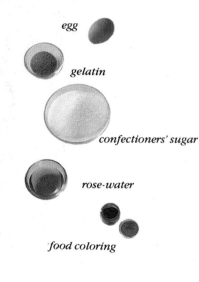

egg

gelatin

confectioners' sugar

rose-water

food coloring

1 Lightly oil an 11 × 7 in jelly roll pan. Sift together the confectioners' sugar and cornstarch and use some of this mixture to coat the inside of the pan evenly. Shake out the excess.

4 Bring the syrup to a boil and boil steadily without stirring until the temperature reaches 260°F on a sugar thermometer. Remove from the heat and stir in the gelatin mixture.

2 Mix together the cold water, rose-water, gelatin and a drop of pink food coloring in a small bowl. Place over a saucepan of hot water and stir occasionally until the gelatin has dissolved.

3 Place the sugar, liquid glucose and boiling water in a heavy-based saucepan. Stir over a low heat to dissolve the sugar completely. Ensure that there are no sugar crystals around the water line; if so, wash these down with a brush dipped in cold water.

5 While the syrup is boiling, whisk the egg whites stiffly in a large bowl using an electric hand whisk. Pour a steady stream of syrup onto the egg whites while whisking continuously for about 3 minutes or until the mixture is thick and foamy. At this stage add more food coloring if the mixture looks too pale.

6 Pour the mixture into the prepared pan and allow to set for about 4 hours or overnight. Sift some of the remaining confectioners' sugar mixture over the surface of the marshmallow and the rest over a board or cookie sheet. Ease the mixture away from the pan using an oiled metal spatula and invert onto the board. Cut into 1 in squares, coating the cut sides with the sugar mixture. Pack into glass containers or tins and seal well.

Glacé Fruits

These luxury sweetmeats are very popular at Christmas and they cost a fraction of the store price if made at home. The whole process takes about 4 weeks, but the result is well worth the effort. Choose one type of fruit, or select a variety of fruits such as cherries, plums, peaches, apricots, star fruit, pineapple, apples, oranges, lemons, limes and clementines.

Makes 24 pieces

INGREDIENTS
1 lb fruit
4½ cups granulated sugar
1 cup powdered glucose

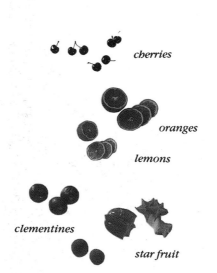

cherries

oranges

lemons

clementines

star fruit

apricots

1 Remove the pits from cherries, plums, peaches and apricots. Peel and core pineapple and cut into cubes or rings. Peel, core and quarter apples and thinly slice citrus fruits. Prick the skins of cherries with a stainless steel needle so the syrup can penetrate the skin.

2 Place enough of the prepared fruit in a saucepan to cover the base, keeping individual fruit types together. Add enough water to cover the fruit and simmer very gently, to avoid breaking it, until almost tender. Use a slotted spoon to lift the fruit and place in a shallow dish, removing any skins if necessary. Repeat as above until all the fruit has been cooked.

3 Measure 1¼ cups of the liquid, or make up this quantity with water if necessary. Pour into the saucepan and add 4 tbsp sugar and the glucose. Heat gently, stirring occasionally, until dissolved. Bring to a boil and pour over the fruit in the dish, completely immersing it, and leave overnight.

4 DAY 2. Drain the syrup from the fruit into the saucepan and add 4 tbsp sugar. Heat gently to dissolve the syrup and bring to a boil. Pour over the fruit and leave overnight. Repeat this process each day, draining off the syrup, dissolving 4 tbsp sugar, boiling the syrup and immersing the fruit and leaving overnight on Days 3, 4, 5, 6 and 7.

5 DAY 8. Drain the fruit, dissolve ½ cup sugar in the syrup and bring to a boil. Add the fruit and cook gently for 3 minutes. Return to the dish and leave for 2 days. DAY 10. Repeat as above for Day 8; at this stage the syrup should look like clear honey. Leave in the dish for at least a further 10 days, or up to 3 weeks.

6 Place a wire rack over a tray and remove each piece of fruit with a slotted spoon. Arrange on the rack. Dry the fruit in a warm dry place or in the oven at the lowest setting until the surface no longer feels sticky. To coat in sugar, spear each piece of fruit and plunge into boiling water, then roll in granulated sugar. To dip into syrup, place the remaining sugar and ¾ cup of water in a saucepan. Heat gently until the sugar has dissolved, then boil for 1 minute. Dip each piece of fruit into boiling water, then quickly into the syrup. Place on the wire rack and leave in a warm place until dry. Place the fruits in paper candy cases and pack into boxes.

Rosehip Cordial

If you get the chance to collect rosehips from the hedges, this cordial makes a wonderfully Christmassy drink. If you can't find rosehips, replace them with black currants.

Makes 7¹/₂ cups

INGREDIENTS
11¼ cups water
6 cups rosehips
4 cups granulated sugar

rosehips

COOK'S TIP

To sterilize, dissolve one crushed water sterilizing tablet in 1 tbsp of boiled water and add to each 2½ cups of cordial. Pour the cordial into the sterilized bottles and seal with a cork or stopper. Store the cordial in the fridge.

1 Sterilize 4 small bottles. Place 7½ cups of water in a large heavy-based saucepan and bring to a boil. Put the rosehips in a food processor and process until finely chopped. Add to the boiling water, bring back to a boil, cover with a lid and turn off the heat. Leave to infuse for 15 minutes.

2 Suspend a jelly bag and place a bowl underneath. Sterilize the jelly bag by pouring boiling water through the bag, then discard the water and replace the bowl. Strain the rosehips through the jelly bag and leave until the pulp is almost dry.

3 Return the pulp to the saucepan with another 3¾ cups of water, bring to a boil, cover and infuse for 10 minutes as above and strain, mixing the 2 juices together. Pour the juices back into a clean saucepan and boil to reduce the mixture by half, to about 4 cups. Stir in the sugar, heat gently until dissolved, then boil for 5 minutes. Sterilize the cordial if it is going to be kept for longer than 4 weeks.

Christmas Spirit

This colorful drink has a sharp but sweet taste. It is excellent served as a winter warmer or after a meal, but it is also good as a summer drink with crushed ice.

Makes 3 cups

INGREDIENTS
2 cups cranberries
2 clementines
2 cups granulated sugar
1 cinnamon stick
2 cups vodka

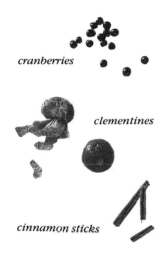

cranberries

clementines

cinnamon sticks

1 Sterilize a large jar and lid. Place the cranberries in a food processor or use a pestle and mortar to crush them evenly. Spoon the cranberries into the jar. Pare the rind thinly from the clementines taking care not to include the white pith. Squeeze the juice and add with the rind to the jar.

2 Add the sugar, cinnamon stick and vodka to the jar and seal with the lid or a double thickness of plastic, and tie down securely. Shake the jar well to combine all the ingredients.

3 Store in a cool place for 1 month, shaking the jar daily for 2 weeks, then occasionally. When the drink has matured, sterilize some small pretty bottles and using a funnel with a filter paper inside, strain the liquid into the bottles and cork immediately. Label clearly and tie a gift tag around the neck.

Festive Liqueurs

These are easier to make than wines and may be made with a variety of flavors and spirits. All these liqueurs should be allowed to mature for 3 months before drinking.

Makes 3¾ cups of each liqueur

PLUM BRANDY
1 lb plums
1 cup raw sugar
2½ cups brandy

FRUIT GIN
3 cups raspberries, black currants or purple plums
1½ cups granulated sugar
3 cups gin

CITRUS WHISKY
1 large orange
1 small lemon
1 lime
1 cup granulated sugar
2½ cups whisky

orange

peaches

lemon

lime

black currants

1 Sterilize 3 jars and lids. Wash and halve the plums, remove the pits and finely slice. Place the plums in the sterilized jar with the sugar and brandy. Crack 3 pits, remove the kernels and chop. Add to the jar and stir until well blended.

2 Place the raspberries, blackcurrants or plums into the prepared jar. If using plums, prick the surface of the fruit using a stainless steel pin to extract its juice. Add the sugar and gin and stir until well blended.

3 To make the Citrus Whisky, first scrub the fruit. Using a sharp knife or potato peeler pare the rind from the fruit, taking care not to include the white pith. Squeeze out all the juice and place in the jar with the fruit rinds. Add the sugar and whisky, stir until well blended.

4 Cover the jars with lids or double thickness plastic tied well down. Store the jars in a cool place for 3 months.

5 Shake the Fruit Gin every day for 1 month, and then occasionally. Shake the Plum Brandy and Citrus Whisky every day for 2 weeks, then occasionally. Sterilize the chosen bottles and corks or stoppers for each liqueur.

6 When each liqueur is ready to be bottled, strain, then pour into the bottles through a funnel fitted with a filter paper. Fit the corks or stoppers and label with a festive label.

INDEX

USEFUL ADDRESSES

Most of the equipment used in this book is available from good kitchen suppliers or large department stores. For more specialized equipment, consult the business directory for addresses in your area.

Bridge Kitchenware
214 East 52nd St
New York, NY 10022
Tel: 212-688-4220
(catalog available)